T0358218

Cambridge Elements

Elements in Language Teaching
edited by
Heath Rose
University of Oxford
Jim McKinley
University College London

PEER ASSESSMENT IN WRITING INSTRUCTION

Shulin Yu
University of Macau

CAMBRIDGE
UNIVERSITY PRESS

Shaftesbury Road, Cambridge CB2 8EA, United Kingdom

One Liberty Plaza, 20th Floor, New York, NY 10006, USA

477 Williamstown Road, Port Melbourne, VIC 3207, Australia

314–321, 3rd Floor, Plot 3, Splendor Forum, Jasola District Centre,
New Delhi – 110025, India

103 Penang Road, #05–06/07, Visioncrest Commercial, Singapore 238467

Cambridge University Press is part of Cambridge University Press & Assessment,
a department of the University of Cambridge.

We share the University's mission to contribute to society through the pursuit of
education, learning and research at the highest international levels of excellence.

www.cambridge.org
Information on this title: www.cambridge.org/9781009475662

DOI: 10.1017/9781009429979

First published 2024

A catalogue record for this publication is available from the British Library

ISBN 978-1-009-47566-2 Hardback
ISBN 978-1-009-42999-3 Paperback
ISSN 2632-4415 (online)
ISSN 2632-4407 (print)

Peer Assessment in Writing Instruction

Elements in Language Teaching

DOI: 10.1017/9781009429979
First published online: January 2024

Shulin Yu
University of Macau

Author for correspondence: Shulin Yu, shulinyu@um.edu.mo

Abstract: This Element traces the evolution of peer assessment in writing instruction and illustrates how peer assessment can be used to promote the teaching and learning of writing in various sociocultural and educational contexts. Specifically, this Element aims to present a critical discussion of the major themes and research findings in existing studies on peer assessment with regard to the three assessment paradigms (assessment of, for, and as learning), and to identify whether and how peer assessment has served the purposes of assessment of, for, and as learning, respectively, in writing instruction. This Element highlights the contextual factors that shape the effect of peer assessment in writing instruction, and concludes with directions for future research and implications regarding how peer assessment can be successfully used to improve students' writing development.

Keywords: peer assessment, peer feedback, writing instruction, second language writing, writing assessment

ISBNs: 9781009475662 (HB), 9781009429993 (PB), 9781009429979 (OC)
ISSNs: 2632-4415 (online), 2632-4407 (print)

Contents

1 Introduction

Over the past decades, peer assessment has been increasingly used as an important strategy and approach for collaborative learning, and is a major assessment activity in writing classrooms in a variety of school and university settings. Peer assessment in the educational context was defined by Topping (2017) as "an arrangement for learners to consider and specify the level, value, or quality of a product or performance of other equal-status learners, then learn further by giving elaborated feedback and discussing their judgments with peers to achieve a negotiated agreed outcome" (p. 1). In writing research, peer assessment has also been referred to as "peer feedback," "peer review," "peer evaluation," and "peer editing." Among the various strands of research across different contexts, it is generally agreed that by definition, peer assessment of writing refers to the use of peers as sources of feedback and interactants, whereby peer learners undertake the roles and responsibilities usually assumed by teachers, or other trained writers or editors, in commenting on each other's drafts in the process of writing (Liu & Hansen Edwards, 2002; Yu & Lee, 2016a).

While various aspects of peer assessment in different writing contexts have been investigated, the research scholarship seems to view peer assessment predominantly as a mechanism of assessment for learning (AfL). There seems to be a portrait of peer assessment as an AfL strategy through which learners use established criteria to tell each other what they have achieved and where improvement is needed. Such a portrait, although underpinned by a range of empirical evidence (for a review, see Vougan & Li, 2022; Yu & Lee, 2016b), risks overlooking or underemphasizing alternative roles that peer assessment might play in learners' writing development. For instance, it is unclear whether and how peer assessment of writing could serve the summative role of measurement and scoring, which is also known as "assessment of learning" (AoL). There is also very limited discussion of whether and how peer assessment could facilitate a recent assessment orientation which places learners at the center of the assessment process, called "assessment as learning" (AaL). Given that the decades-long assessment research has given rise to three major paradigms of assessment, that is, AoL, AfL, and AaL (Earl, 2013), and that the use of peer assessment has taken on different forms for diverse purposes across different contexts, including but not limited to the first language (L1) writing context and English as a second/foreign language (L2) context, a systemic and comprehensive discussion of peer assessment of writing in relation to the three assessment paradigms in different contexts is warranted.

The aim of this Element is therefore to present a critical discussion of the major themes and research findings in existing studies on peer assessment with regard to the three assessment paradigms, and to identify whether and how peer assessment has served the purposes of assessment of, for, and as learning, respectively, in writing instruction. More specifically, this Element aims to illustrate how peer assessment can play a role in the summative evaluation of student writing ability, reveal how peer assessment can generate feedback for teachers to enhance their instruction and for students to improve their writing, and demonstrate how peer assessment enables students to develop their cognitive and metacognitive capacities in self-evaluating their writing ability and self-regulating their writing process and performance. By situating the roles of peer assessment of writing in not only individual learner factors, but also sociocultural contexts, this Element also intends to illustrate what and how contextual factors, if any, shape the effectiveness of peer assessment in serving formative, summative, and metacognitive purposes in learners' writing development. This Element is significant since it synthesizes the salient issues that have been explored in existing research on peer assessment in writing and identifies research gaps and further research directions. It also offers implications for classroom practices to bridge the gap between research and practice with regard to the implementation of peer assessment in writing classrooms.

In the next sections, I will first introduce a conceptual framework used to inform the analysis of the published literature on peer assessment in writing instruction. Then I will present the major themes and findings of peer assessment research in different sociocultural and educational contexts, including L1 writing, English as a Second Language (ESL)/English as a Foreign Language (EFL) university writing, English for Academic Purposes (EAP)/English for Specific Purposes (ESP) writing contexts, ESL/EFL school writing, and non-English foreign language writing. I will conclude this Element by discussing how to move forward with research on peer assessment in writing instruction and how to bridge possible gaps between research and practice in peer assessment in writing instruction.

2 Conceptual Framework: Peer Assessment of, for and as Learning in Writing Classrooms

This section provides a conceptual framework that illustrates the different roles and functions of peer assessment in writing classrooms. Depending on its purpose, classroom assessment of writing can be conceptualized as a continuum of three major approaches: assessment of learning (AoL), assessment for learning (AfL), and assessment as learning (AaL) (Earl, 2013; Lee, 2017) (see Figure 1). The AoL approach to writing assessment has a strong summative orientation, which views writing primarily as a product and focuses on student scores for administrative and reporting purposes (Lee, 2017). Such an approach is particularly common in contexts of high-stakes testing culture and the Confucian heritage culture, within which teachers are normally viewed as authorities of feedback provision and

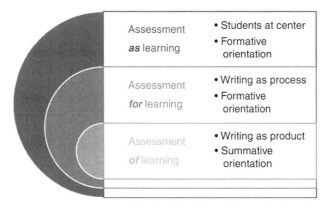

Figure 1 Assessment of, for, and as learning and writing instruction.

students merely as passive recipients of writing knowledge and teacher feedback. Overall, AoL mainly views assessment as measurement, which is underpinned by the philosophical belief that knowledge exists separately from the learner, who then works hard to consume and acquire it rather than to construct it (Serafini, 2001).

In contrast, AfL has a formative orientation, focusing on the improvement of teaching and learning (Black & William, 2009). An AfL approach to writing assessment aims to identify students' strengths and weaknesses in writing through quality feedback. Different from AoL, students and teachers share responsibilities through participating in the assessment and feedback process (Lee, 2017). Teachers no longer play a dominant role but become mediators "in enhancing student learning" (Carless, 2007, p. 172). An AfL approach to writing assessment focuses mainly on writing as a process, during which learners are given opportunities to engage with assessment activities such as peer assessment or portfolio assessment. In an AfL-based writing classroom, writing teachers elaborate on success criteria and writing goals, while students engage in peer assessment activities and give constructive feedback to their peers.

The AaL approach extends the role of formative assessment and further places students at the center of assessment (Schellekens et al., 2021). According to Earl (2013), AaL is "a subset of AfL but it emphasizes the important role of students as active agents in the assessment process" (p. 553). Different from AfL, which focuses on the role of teachers in designing appropriate assessment tasks, AaL intends to empower students to be reflective and active learners who can identify their own strengths and weaknesses, set up their own learning goals, and monitor and regulate their own learning and writing progress through a range of strategies (Lee, 2017; Schellekens et al., 2021). The AaL approach to writing assessment enables student writers to make use of cognitive and metacognitive resources to recognize their writing problems, identify the nature of the writing problems, use strategies to resolve the problems and improve their writing, and evaluate their writing behaviors, process, and performance. The ultimate goal of the AaL approach in writing classrooms is to develop student writers' self-regulation and metacognitive abilities for lifelong learning and personal development (Lee et al., 2019; Li et al., 2022; Zimmerman & Schunk, 2008).

Despite their different roles and purposes in assessment, AoL, AfL, and AaL are not mutually exclusive because assessment can serve both summative and formative purposes, and there are overlapping functions among the three assessment paradigms (Lee, 2017; Schellekens et al., 2021). For example, peer assessment can take many forms and be used for both summative and formative purposes depending on learning goals and disciplinary and institutional contexts. Chin and colleagues (2015) described peer assessment's positive impact on "assessment of/for/as learning" practices: Peer feedback not only improves students' writing performance as a whole (AoL), but also promotes their critical reasoning and evaluative judgment as students need to consider the validity and appropriateness of peers' comments and decide whether to accept them or not (AaL); the promoted critical reasoning will in turn improve students' writing as writing is an act of discovering meaning (AfL). Summative peer assessment normally refers to peer grading, in which students evaluate their peers' work and assign grades based on assessment rubrics and criteria. Apart from peer grading, students can also provide formative and constructive feedback on their peers' drafts. Such formative peer assessment can be done as in-class activities or using online feedback tools. Peer feedback/assessment, "as a major peer activity for learning in L2 writing classes" (Yu & Lee, 2016a, p. 461), has been extensively promulgated for teachers to enhance their instruction and for students to improve their L2 writing.

Research has also shown that peer assessment can offer opportunities for students to learn to set personal learning goals and monitor their learning during the revision process (Lee et al., 2019; Topping, 2009). As peer assessors and feedback givers, students can participate in the assessment and learning activities as active agents who take responsibility for their own learning through exercising autonomy and self-reflection in learning (Gao et al., 2017; Huisman et al., 2018; Topping et al., 2000). Apart from learner independence, researchers and practitioners in writing instruction and assessment have realized the importance of peer assessment in improving learning via peer interactions and peer scaffolding. Peer assessment *as* learning in writing classrooms considers how student writers self-regulate their own writing processes and performances in assessment situations, as well as using their cognitive and metacognitive capacities to make complex decisions regarding how they use peer assessment and engage with the writing tasks and activities (Dann, 2014).

Nevertheless, although there are a number of studies on peer assessment in various writing contexts, a systemic investigation of the issues relating to purposes, topics, and designs in peer assessment research across different contexts through the lens of the three assessment paradigms (AoL, AfL, and AaL) is still lacking. This research inadequacy makes it difficult to understand what and how the varied assessment paradigms have informed peer assessment research. By situating peer assessment within the three assessment paradigms, this Element intends to provide a conceptual framework that reveals the cycle of teaching, learning, and peer assessment in different writing instructional contexts (i.e., L1 writing, ESL/EFL university writing, ESL/EFL school writing, non-English foreign language writing, and EAP/ESP writing contexts) and to highlight the role and functions of peer assessment in writing instruction (see Figure 2). In the sections that follow, I will describe how peer assessment serves AoL, AfL, and AaL purposes in each of the aforementioned writing contexts.

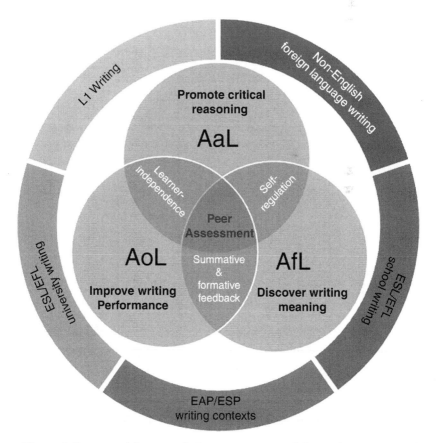

Figure 2 Conceptual framework: Peer assessment of, for, and as learning in writing classrooms.

3 Peer Assessment in the L1 Writing Context

The contexts of research on peer assessment in L1 writing vary considerably, from secondary schools (Sadler & Good, 2006) to postgraduate programs (Pope, 2001). Three research paradigms were found among the research on peer feedback in L1 writing, with AfL dominating the whole process. Earlier research on peer feedback used AoL more often, while later researchers have tended to shift to AaL.

3.1 Peer Assessment of Learning

Not surprisingly, few research studies have used an AoL perspective to examine the reliability and validity of peer assessment in the teaching and learning of writing in L1 contexts (Anson & Anson, 2017; Cho & MacArthur, 2010; Cho, Schunn, & Charney, 2006; Patchan et al., 2009). Two early studies were conducted to examine how peer assessment could play a role in the summative evaluation of students' writing abilities (Cho, Schunn, & Charney, 2006; Sadler & Good, 2006). The researchers developed scoring rubrics to scaffold peer assessment and aimed to reveal the differences in writing instructors' and students' assessments of writing. Cho, Schunn, and Wilson (2006) compared teachers' and students' perspectives regarding the reliability and validity of 708 peer-generated writing scores in the US context. Each student was required to write two drafts on which five to six peers and an instructor provided summative assessment in three dimensions on a seven-point Likert scale. Sadler and Good (2006) compared teacher-generated grades with those awarded by peers and students themselves in the context of a middle school science classroom. Though both studies were situated in the US context, they revealed contrasting results. In the first study, instructors and students were found to have opposite perceptions regarding the reliability and validity of peer ratings, with instructors being quite positive and students being very negative. Students perceived peer assessment "to be more noise than signal" (Cho, Schunn, & Wilson, 2006, p. 898). However, in the other study, high correlations ($r = 0.91$ to 0.94) were found among grades generated by teachers, peers, and students themselves (Sadler & Good, 2006). The researchers attributed the contrasting results to the restricted information received by the students, arguing that the limited number of ratings available to students led to lower reliability and validity (Cho, Schunn, & Wilson, 2006).

Apart from using peer assessment simply as a tool for summative evaluation, Sadler and Good (2006) took a step forward to investigate the extent to which peer grading and self-grading would lead to better learning. The results showed that compared with peer grading, self-grading facilitated student understanding to a greater extent. Although metacognitive learning was not investigated in the study, the researchers were aware that students had opportunities to "reflect on the activity of grading others or themselves in writing" (p. 25). Cho, Schunn, and Wilson (2006) also carefully constructed assessment rubrics and provided students with detailed instructions on how to use the rubrics for peer assessment. Students were appropriately scaffolded throughout the process, in which they could learn from examining their peers' problems and comparing their own writing with others. These early attempts provided the research rationale for subsequent studies, demonstrating that peer feedback, as an important alternative to teacher feedback, can be used in educational settings.

Patchan and colleagues (2009) compared the comments produced by students, content instructors, and writing instructors and found that both student and teacher feedback commented on a significant number of ideas, which provided empirical evidence supporting the validity of peer feedback. In terms of their differences, students used praise twice as much as the instructors. Higher-proficient peer reviewers were found to use mitigating strategies when giving criticism, which was not found in any instructor comments. Their study also revealed that content instructors tended to be more problem focused, while writing instructors were more solution oriented. The authors suggested that students focused more on content issues, whereas instructors paid more attention to the negative emotional impact of criticism and offered more solutions and explanations.

Scholars in this line of research further examined how different sources of feedback relate to students' revision and writing quality. In doing so, a quasi-experimental study was conducted. Cho and MacArthur (2010) divided twenty-eight undergraduate students into three groups, in which students received feedback from a single expert, a single peer, or multiple peers separately. The study revealed that the group that received comments from multiple peers improved the most in writing performance. It lends further empirical support to the adoption of peer feedback in writing, demonstrating that "at least under some conditions, students are able to provide useful feedback to their peers without training in evaluation" (p. 335). Patchan and colleagues (2011) took a different perspective, investigating how students' writing was influenced by different evaluators (i.e., teaching assistants and peers) in an undergraduate natural science course. Students tended to perform better and produce more revisions when the evaluators of their writing were peers, although there was only a moderate difference in the quality of final drafts. Intergroup comparisons were also found between L1 and L2 speakers. In his doctoral dissertation, Kim (2012) compared the peer feedback generated by L1 and L2 university students in three peer assessment sessions over an academic semester. Both inter-language and cross-session comparisons were conducted. The results showed that L1 and L2 writers generally provided similar amounts and types of feedback. Students who improved in writing made more revisions by adding and deleting idea chunks, while the less-improved students received more general criticism. It seems that specific suggestions are more helpful for students to make improvements in their writing.

In general, these comparative studies lend empirical support to the use of peer assessment and grading as a summative assessment strategy in L1 writing classrooms. Feedback generated from peer assessment activities that features more praise, nondirective feedback, and mitigating strategies has been perceived to be useful and reader friendly (Cho & MacArthur, 2010; Cho, Schunn, & Charney, 2006; Patchan et al., 2009).

3.2 Peer Assessment for Learning

The majority of previous studies on peer assessment in L1 writing have adopted an AfL paradigm to investigate how the formative use of peer assessment results in students' improvement in writing. The research in this paradigm can be broadly divided into three strands: the first strand of research focused on students' perceptions of the formative peer review experience (e.g., Bauer et al., 2009); the second group of studies designed and implemented various pedagogical interventions in the process of formative peer assessment (e.g., Wooley, 2007); and the third strand examined the relationship between various types of peer feedback and students' uptake and text revisions (e.g., Nelson & Schunn, 2009).

The first strand of studies mainly concerns students' perceptions regarding peer assessment practice. In this line of research, participants were asked to provide comments on their peers' writing. Follow-up interviews, reflections, or questionnaires were assigned to reveal students' perceptions of their peer evaluation experience. For example, contextualized in an Australian university, Pope (2001) used the business theory of consumption values as the theoretical framework to examine postgraduate students' experiences of giving peer evaluation. The findings suggest that the use of peer evaluation helps to improve students' writing and reporting skills. Students attributed their learning gains to both assessing their peers' writing and being assessed by their peers. Another study, situated in Austria, used online questionnaires to investigate how students taking a scientific writing course perceived the process, content, and effects of peer review (Bauer et al., 2009). The study concluded that peer reviews led to students' improvement in understanding the essential elements of academic writing, awareness of writing quality, and reflection on their own writing performance (Bauer et al., 2009). Ludemann and McMakin (2014) examined students' perceptions of the value of peer review activities among university freshmen in the US context. The results indicated that students viewed providing peer evaluation as more helpful than receiving peer feedback. A more recent study by Ozkul (2017) investigated undergraduate students' revision practices after receiving peer feedback. Reflection essays that provide prompts regarding peer review experiences were assigned to the participants. These reflection essays were qualitatively analyzed and coded to reveal students' perceptions.

With the development of technology and its possibility for improving language teaching and learning, language educators started to apply technology to peer review in writing contexts. For example, Ahmed and Abdu (2021) explored the perceptions of and attitudes toward peer feedback in face-to-face and online conditions. Responses from 142 students and 20 instructors revealed that face-to-face peer feedback was more popular among participants, while online peer feedback was perceived as less effective as they preferred to receive immediate feedback from peers directly. Similarly, Latifi and colleagues' (2021) study, situated in an online context, investigated students' perceptions of the effectiveness of different types of online peer feedback. They found that student writers were generally in favor of online peer feedback with scripts or guided support in contrast to unscripted situations, and they perceived that the former two forms of online peer feedback could contribute to both domain-general and domain-specific academic progress. Overall, these studies found that L1 writers generally have positive perceptions of peer assessment, and peer feedback is considered helpful in their learning process.

Over the past two decades, researchers have also been interested in designing different pedagogical interventions of peer assessment and examining their effects on students' writing performance. Wooley (2007) examined differences in writing quality between students who were required to provide peer feedback prior to their own writing and those who wrote without such a requirement. The results indicated that students who provided elaborate feedback outperformed those who only provided numerical ratings to their peers' writing. This finding did not hold true in some later studies. Strijbos and colleagues (2010) investigated the impact of feedback content (concise general or elaborate specific) and feedback providers' competence levels on students' feedback perception and performance in the EAP context. Contrary to the findings of Wooley (2007), elaborate specific feedback by a more proficient peer led to a more negative effect, whereas students who received concise general feedback performed significantly better. Apart from these two studies, researchers also compared the impacts of different instructional supports on peer feedback in online settings. Latifi and colleagues (2021) conducted an intergroup comparison in an online peer feedback platform by randomly dividing learners into three groups with different levels of support for providing peer feedback (i.e., guided, scripted, and unscripted peer feedback). The findings showed that students in the scripted group presented the best quality of writing, followed by the guided group and the unscripted group. The results were the same for feedback quality among the three groups.

In terms of the effects of peer reviewing on student revision, Covill (2010) compared the effects of three revision approaches (i.e., formal peer review, no formal review, and formal self-review) on students' revision and writing per-formance. The results showed that the no formal review group made the most revisions throughout the whole writing process and held the most positive attitude toward the writing instruction. However, in a more recent study, Baker (2016) required students to provide feedback on each other's writing drafts four weeks ahead of the submission deadline. The comparison between the first draft and final essay showed positive results. The majority of students added more than 50 percent new material and made major revisions to the final essay. Most of the revisions belong to the category of meaning-level changes (78.9 percent), whereas only 21.1 percent of the changes were categorized as surface-level revisions. The results suggest that students were highly engaged with peer feedback and were willing to make revisions.

A small number of studies adopted a correlational design to explore how different factors (such as feedback types) relate to students' revision and writing quality. For example, a study conducted by Huisman and colleagues (2017) examined whether different groupings (homogeneous or heterogeneous recip-rocal dyads) would influence students' writing performance. Adopting a quasi-experimental design, they found that individual ability or dyad composition was not directly related to writing performance. Also, neither of the two variables predicted feedback quality (i.e., the usefulness and effectiveness of the feed-back). A more recent correlational study took the type of peer feedback activ-ities into consideration and examined their influences on students' writing revision and learning (Wu & Schunn, 2023). Writing samples and revisions collected from 367 students were compared and analyzed after three types of learning activities: constructive activity (i.e., providing explanations and mak-ing revisions after receiving feedback), active activity (i.e., making revisions after receiving feedback), and passive activity (i.e., receiving feedback without revising). The findings showed that those activities resulted in different learning outcomes for students, where constructive activities were most related to learning to write, while the other two kinds of activities had a weaker relationship with it.

Individual differences (e.g., gender) have also been considered as factors influencing peer reviewers' writing and feedback quality. Another study conducted by Leung and colleagues (2010) adopted a qualitative approach to explore the role of gender in the quality and types of feedback in the context of e-feedback. The analysis showed that male peer reviewers were more likely to provide specific comments and suggestions than their female counterparts.

3.3 Peer Assessment as Learning

A few studies have looked into how participation in peer assessment could improve students' cognitive and metacognitive development in their writing abilities and in what ways peer assessment could enhance feedback givers' writing performance. Althauser and Darnall (2001) conducted early research that investigated how student participation, responsiveness, the quality of peer feedback provided, and the quality of peer feedback received related to a student's own writing performance. The results showed that the quality of peer feedback provided significantly influenced the students' writing quality throughout the whole process, whereas the quality of feedback received only affected writing quality in the last round of peer reviewing. The authors suggested that "self-assistance" or "self-instruction" (Tharp & Gallimore, 1988, pp. 87–91) had a great influence on students' learning performance. When students were involved in active learning, they were more likely to gain cognitive development and acquire metacognitive strategies.

The influence of feedback roles on writing quality was explored in greater detail in a later study by Li and colleagues (2010). The study explored the relationship between the quality of student projects and the quality of peer assessment in a technology application course. Forty-three teacher education students were first required to comment on and rate two peer projects, and then were required to revise their own work based on the feedback received. Students' first draft and final assignments were evaluated by two independent raters. The results suggested that when the quality of the initial projects was controlled, there was a high correlation between the quality of peer feedback provided and the quality of the students' final writing. In contrast, the researchers found no significant correlation between the quality of the received peer feedback and the quality of their writing. This echoes Althauser and Darnall's (2001) study, suggesting that active engagement in reviewing facilitates student learning. Some explanations were provided for the results.

Students were not told to accept the feedback without distinction. Instead, they were encouraged to obtain a better understanding of the content and the rubrics before making revisions. The peer assessment process enables students to learn to evaluate their own projects and make informed decisions about revision.

McConlogue (2015) conducted a case study to explore a peer assessor's whole process of composing and receiving peer feedback. In line with previous research, the student participant considered the process of providing feedback positive while viewing receiving feedback as negative. In the process of evaluating her peers' reports, the participant seemed to be "benchmarking her report against her peers, checking where her report fit in and what she could improve on" (p. 1501). Apparently, this active learning involvement gave a "joyful experience" to the student. Arguably, the student developed her understanding of quality through reading, thinking, and evaluating peers' work. In this way, her assessment literacy was cultivated. In contrast, major problems emerged when the participant tried to understand peers' feedback on her writing. She felt that peers' comments were sometimes wrong, which resulted in her losing trust in peer comments. The authors stated that the process of assessing others' work, articulating judgments, and giving feedback could help the peer assessor critically evaluate and assess her own work and identify areas to improve. While making judgments on peers' work, she also learned to draw on a large number of resources, not limited to the guidance and materials the tutor provided. These cognitive and metacognitive developments facilitated the student's self-evaluation and assessment when writing her own essays.

Given the multiple learning benefits brought by feedback provision, Cho and Cho (2011) focused on peer reviewers' learning from evaluating peer drafts in the reciprocal peer assessment activity. Undergraduate students in a scientific writing course took part in the study, in which they were required to review three or four peer drafts, and revise their own drafts accordingly. Feedback segments were analyzed from two dimensions: scope (surface, micro-meaning, and macro-meaning) and evaluation (strength vs. weakness). It was found that providing strength and weakness evaluations on both micro- and macro-meaning levels positively influenced students' own revisions. The authors argued that providing peer reviews enabled students to take a different perspective and anticipate how the readers would interpret their own writing. Thus, reader awareness was cultivated. Meanwhile, student reviewers gained a better understanding of effective writing strategies and assessment rubrics. These learning gains finally led to improvements in writing quality. Moreover, students also benefited from receiving comments on their weaknesses. By commenting on the weaknesses of peer drafts, students gained knowledge of writing constraints that then "help the reviewers to monitor and regulate their own writing" (p. 639). However, providing feedback on surface features did not seem to affect students' revisions. The authors attributed this finding to the fact that L1 university students generally had sufficient basic writing knowledge and skills so that they may not learn much by giving feedback on surface features.

To summarize, peer assessment has been shown to be highly reliable and valid, making them a valuable supplement for teacher feedback in L1 writing contexts (e.g., Patchan et al., 2009). The AfL paradigm has been used in a large proportion of peer assessment studies in such contexts. Peer assessment is generally regarded favorably by students (e.g., Pope, 2001), and peer feedback has been approved to help students enhance their writing quality (e.g., Cho & MacArthur, 2010). Although there are relatively fewer studies that adopted the AaL paradigm, these studies illustrated how providing and receiving peer feedback facilitates students' cognitive and metacognitive development, which finally leads to improved writing quality. Providing peer reviews appears to facilitate writing improvement to a greater extent in comparison with receiving peer reviews. The researchers seem to agree that providing feedback involves students in active learning and leads to greater engagement, which are prerequisites to learning improvement.

4 Peer Assessment in the ESL/EFL University Writing Context

In general, most of the peer assessment research has been conducted in the ESL/ EFL university writing context. For the purposes of this Element, three research foci were synthesized based on the empirical studies within this context. Similar to peer assessment in the L1 writing context, AfL was the most frequent perspective among the current studies, while the research trend gradually shifted from AoL to AaL.

4.1 Peer Assessment of Learning

As an important paradigm in language testing and assessment, assessment *of* learning focuses on the use of assessment to make judgments about student learning and utilize the assessment information for summative reports (Lee & Coniam, 2013; Sadeghi & Rahmati, 2017). Peer assessment *of* learning in L2 writing, accordingly, focuses on using peer assessment in summative evaluation of students' L2 writing ability. While a number of studies have attempted to investigate the appropriateness of peer review as a form of assessment in higher education (e.g., Egan & Costello, 2016; Meek et al., 2017), relatively scant research attention has been paid to L2 writing students. This is partially due to the difficulties of implementing peer assessment as the summative evaluation that usually serves administrative and reporting purposes through grades and scores, involving teachers and university internal or external examination bodies as assessors (Sadeghi & Rahmati, 2017). Coupled with these difficulties is the observation that in traditional L2 writing classrooms, teachers primarily play the role of an assessor and writing assessment primarily serves an AoL purpose (Lee, 2007; Lee & Coniam, 2013).

In the university context, Zhao (2018) found EFL writing teachers were reluctant to use peer assessment as a means of summative evaluation due to their narrow understanding of peer assessment, perceptions of its inappropriateness for EFL writing instruction, constraints of students' writing proficiency and motivation, and perceived conflict of peer assessment with the existing teacher-driven culture of learning. Moreover, in terms of peer and teacher ratings on EFL writing, Rezaei and Barkaoui (2021) found that peers and teachers had various degrees of strictness in both high- and low-stakes writing conditions. Students were stricter on their grades for language use, while teachers were stricter on the organization, and such divergence in rating criteria happened across the groups. From a social-affective perspective, students also expressed dissatisfaction with both the content and scores in the peer assessment process and demonstrated resistance toward peer assessment as a form of summative evaluation (Zhou et al., 2020). Given these difficulties and divergences, traditions, and reluctance, peer assessment has a limited role to play in the summative evaluation of university students' L2 writing ability.

4.2 Peer Assessment for Learning

From a peer-assessment-*for*-learning perspective, the benefits, opportunities, and affordances of peer assessment for learning are mainly manifested in students' writing improvement (Lu et al., 2021). Although peer assessment fits well with a number of theories in writing, education, and second language acquisition (Yu & Lee, 2016a), the literature yields inconclusive results regarding the extent to which it facilitates the improvement of university students' L2 writing quality and how it does so. Some early studies have doubted the effectiveness of peer assessment and indicated that teacher assessment and feedback are more reliable and useful, especially in EFL and ESL contexts (e.g., Nelson & Carson, 1998; Zhang, 1995). Recent research, on the other hand, suggests that teacher, peer, and self-feedback should be integrated into L2 writing instruction because they can play different roles in improving student writing proficiency and peer feedback can have a significant positive overall effect on students' writing (e.g., Birjandi & Tamjid, 2012; Lam, 2013; Vougan & Li, 2022; Yu & Lee, 2016).

Peer assessment in the university context has been studied in comparison with other means of assessing L2 writing, including teacher feedback (Miao et al., 2006; Min, 2018; Nguyen, 2018; Ruegg, 2015, 2018; Tai et al., 2015; Wu et al., 2022), self-feedback (Lu et al., 2021; Wei et al., 2022; Zou et al., 2022), Automated Writing Evalution (AWE) feedback (Chen & Cui, 2022), and peer feedback conference (Zaccaron & Xhafaj, 2020). Peer feedback has been viewed as an effective and reliable supplement to teacher feedback in EFL writing classrooms to collectively improve students' writing accuracy (Nguyen, 2018; Wu et al., 2022). Through combining both, teachers' intervention has been found to have a significant positive impact on students' adoption of various peer feedback types and on their self-revision of writing texts (Sun & Wang, 2022). Studies that reported the contributing effects of peer assessments on improving students' revision and writing quality constitute positive evidence concerning the learning benefits of peer assessment. For instance, the study by Meletiadou (2021b) found that the addition of peer assessment improved students' writing quality in terms of lexical and grammatical complexity and accuracy. The benefits derived from embedding grammatical and lexical aspects in peer assessment are further corroborated by the study of Shang (2022), where online peer feedback seemed to be more useful than automated feedback in improving students' grammatical and lexical aspects of writing. Furthermore, Rezai et al. (2022) focused on the role of online peer assessment in improving students' writing skills through a pre- and post-test design, finding that students' writing skills improved significantly in the post-tests and delayed post-tests. The findings of these studies highlight the significant role of peer assessment in enhancing students' revision processes and writing quality in both online and traditional EFL contexts.

Driven by a growing recognition that both peer and self-assessment can be alternative assessment methods to teacher assessment in the university context, research has also compared the validity and usefulness of the two methods (e.g., Bouziane & Zyad, 2018; Wanner & Palmer, 2018). For example, Lu et al. (2021) conducted a comparative study on the effects of self-feedback and peer feedback on Hong Kong undergraduate students' writing and found that peer feedback had a more significant effect on their writing improvement than self-feedback. Furthermore, peer feedback activity is not limited to pairs. Peer conferences in groups have been regarded as an opportunity for students to elucidate feedback issues, and their feeling of deindividuation enabled them to generate more feedback as anonymous reviewers in the peer groups (Zaccaron & Xhafaj, 2020). Therefore, scholars have called for the careful design and implementation of peer feedback in formative assessment processes in L2 writing, with adequate training on improving writing and its revision quality (Min, 2018; Zhang & Yu, 2022).

Under this line of research, scholars have compared the effects of trained and untrained peer assessment. For example, Min (2006) explored the effects of trained peer assessment on EFL students' subsequent revisions and writing quality in Taiwan. She found that the trained students could learn from peer assessment training in improving their writing skills and language acquisition. Further, other researchers have discussed the effect of peer assessment in relation to the writing and assessing process (e.g., Baker, 2016), maintaining that peer assessment can be more effective at improving students' writing performance if they can actively engage in constructing the criteria-based rubrics (Bouziane & Zyad, 2018). This was based on empirical evidence showing that ESL students who participated in the rubric development process outperformed those who only applied the rubric (Becker, 2016).

Aiming at revealing the role of peer assessment in writing learning, classroom studies of university students have been conducted in L2 contexts to examine what they gained from providing and receiving peer feedback. Cao et al. (2019) found that undergraduate students' learning (or not learning) from receiving and giving peer comments in L2 writing was mediated by student engagement with evaluation criteria, their motivation for peer feedback, their individual differences in writing proficiency, and group dynamics. Yu (2019) further uncovered postgraduate students' learning from providing peer feedback on their theses, and found that participation in peer assessment could raise postgraduate students' genre awareness of academic writing, improve their academic writing skills, and help them become more reflective and critical academic writers. Through learning from receiving and giving peer feedback, L2 writers could not only polish their writing skills but also acquire the academic competence to cope with their various writing tasks.

Some researchers have moved their attention from peer assessment's learning potential to its effectiveness in various L2 writing modes, especially those of online or technology-assisted peer feedback for L2 writing learners (Cao et al., 2022; Chen, 2016; Pham, 2022; Saeed, Ghazali, & Aljaberi, 2018; Tan et al., 2022; Zhang & Zou, 2022). In this vein, Cao et al. (2022) synthesized that students who received online peer feedback could outperform those who received offline peer feedback in many aspects of ESL/EFL writing, including writing performance, learning environment, and writing attitudes and motivation. For example, experimental procedures have revealed the impact of synchronous discussion on EFL undergraduates' writing performance in web-based peer assessment (Liu et al., 2018; Zheng et al., 2018). To further reveal the role of different online assessment methods, researchers have uncovered the effectiveness of affective, cognitive, and metacognitive feedback (Cheng et al., 2015), rating plus qualitative feedback within an online environment (Xiao & Lucking, 2008), various feedback formats and executive thinking styles (Lin et al., 2001) as well as the benefits of peer feedback for L2 writing beyond institutional space, such as in a Facebook group (Saeed, Ghazali, Sahuri, & Abdulrab, 2018) or on a Wiki platform (Ma, 2020).

Furthermore, technology-assisted peer feedback has been found to have a positive effect on the construction of L2 knowledge (Shang, 2022; Tran & Pham, 2023; Zhang & Zou, 2022) and academic knowledge in L2 writing (Yang, 2016). Shang (2022) found that online peer feedback is more effective in improving EFL learners' writing at the sentence level. For academic knowledge, through taking part in peer feedback on a computer-supported collaborative learning (CSCL) system, EFL postgraduate students were able to generate more local (i.e., grammatical) and global revisions (i.e., text development and organization) on both their own and their peers' writing. Sun and Zhang (2022) investigated the potential impact of translanguaging in the process of online peer feedback on L2 students' writing performance. They discovered that compared with English-only online peer feedback, translanguaging online peer feedback was more conducive to improving learners' L2 writing performance, and their study also revealed that writing instructors need to take a few factors such as motivation, agency, self-efficacy, and translanguaging awareness into consideration in order to enhance students' translanguaging practice in peer assessment.

In short, studies in this line of research have expanded the topic of peer assessment *for* learning from the primary focus on the effectiveness of peer assessment on the improvement of L2 writing situated in face-to-face classrooms to further discussion on the optimization of peer assessment in various modes so that it can be used as a means to enhance teacher instruction and student writing proficiency beyond traditional writing classrooms.

4.3 Peer Assessment as Learning

From a peer-assessment-*as*-learning perspective, extant studies have focused on: (1) the effect of peer assessment on changes in students' writing self-efficacy and (2) the effect of peer assessment on students' cognitive and metacognitive capacities in self-evaluating their L2 writing ability. Research exploring the effect of peer assessment on students' writing self-efficacy has been informed by theories in education, psychology, and second language acquisition that view self-efficacy as a key factor leading to successful language learning (Lee & Evans, 2019; Ruegg, 2018). It is argued that students' self-efficacy beliefs can be developed through verbal persuasion that, in turn, can be realized through peer assessment (Pajares, 2003; Schunk & Swartz, 1993).

However, empirical research on the effects of peer assessment on writing self-efficacy has provided inconsistent findings. Ruegg (2010, 2018) investigated the effects of peer feedback on Japanese university students' EFL writing self-efficacy. She found that while peer feedback was the only variable that predicted students' increased confidence when they received both peer and teacher feedback, the self-efficacy of students who received peer feedback increased far less than that of those who received teacher feedback. Conversely, Lee and Evans (2019) indicated that undergraduate students who received either face-to-face or online peer feedback demonstrated improvements in writing self-efficacy, and they perceived that giving (but not receiving) peer feedback enhanced writing self-efficacy directly through the mediation of writing self-regulatory efficacy and apprehension. A recent study conducted by Cui et al. (2022) revealed that teacher feedback and trained peer feedback had similar positive effects on students' enhancement of writing competence and writing self-efficacy, while trained peer feedback contributed to a more significant improvement of students' autonomous motivation than teacher feedback. In terms of students' autonomy, inconsistent findings have uncovered changes (or no change) in students' writing self-efficacy after providing and receiving peer feedback and the potential of peer assessment to be implemented as AaL in students' regulation of their L2 writing learning. Thus, future empirical studies are needed to explore how peer assessment plays a role in influencing writing self-efficacy beliefs, taking into consideration the relevant individual differences and contextual factors.

Another string of studies uncovered that peer assessment affects university students' cognitive and metacognitive development through embedded social interactions (Carson & Nelson, 1994; Yu & Lee, 2016b), assistance of technology (Zhang & Zou, 2022; Zou et al., 2022), or implementing peer feedback activities in the online context (Pham et al., 2020; Tian et al., 2022). Peer assessment activities in L2 writing gave students new opportunities to "develop and investigate their thoughts, understand the right terms to convey their thoughts, and discuss these thoughts with their readers" (Huang, 2015, p. 1), which will in turn foster their cognitive development and metacognitive feedback awareness and strategies in addition to their writing performance and skills (Zheng et al., 2018).

However, given the fact that previous research has yielded inconsistent findings regarding the effectiveness of peer feedback (as noted earlier in this section), some researchers have contended that the positive effect of peer feedback on students' cognitive development would not be fully realized unless the issues regarding peer feedback quality and efficiency are addressed (Zhang & Zou, 2022). For example, Lee (2015) contended that the key issue should be soliciting quality feedback from the reviewers, and support should be given to the student reviewers in terms of their cognitive and psychological functioning. Conversely, Zhang and McEneaney (2020) stated that despite the quality of reviewers' feedback and receivers' responses being significant predictors of writing performance, the quality of authors' responses had a slightly more significant impact than the quality of reviewers' feedback. These results demonstrate that peer assessment, as a formative learning approach, could strengthen both feedback givers and receivers' cognitive and metacognitive development in writing when its quality can be guaranteed. Therefore, scholars have appealed for several means of training to cultivate favorable attitudes toward peer review, polish the peer feedback response with strategic guidance or evaluation, and develop L2 writers with sufficient self-efficacy and self-regulation skills (Lee, 2015; Zhang & McEneaney, 2020).

Moreover, Ramon-Casas et al. (2019) found that lower-achieving students' writing skills increased more as a result of participating in peer assessment than their more accomplished peers. Their analysis showed that peer assessment is oriented toward learning, with the researchers crediting the opportunity for lower-achieving students to engage in metacognitive reflection on their own work while evaluating their peers' work for the positive effects of peer assessment on these students' self-regulated learning. Additionally, Zheng et al. (2018) examined the effects of synchronous discussion between peer assessors and assessees on writing quality, qualitative feedback quality, self-efficacy, and metacognitive awareness in web-based peer assessment, and they revealed that the experiment group participating in peer assessment with synchronous discussion showed more improvement in writing performance, metacognitive awareness, and self-efficacy. Moreover, Lin's (2019) study focused on comparing the effects of online peer assessment and conventional peer assessment on students' learning achievement, involvement, and autonomy; the analysis reflected orientations toward both AfL and AaL. This study revealed that the online peer assessment group appeared to outperform the tradition peer assessment group in given aspects of learning achievement and autonomy, indicating that peer assessment is not merely viewed as a feedback tool to promote students' writing but rather as a process whereby students' reflection and autonomy can be boosted as well. Similarly, Shen et al. (2020) also offered convincing evidence for the role of peer assessment in increasing students' learning autonomy. These results demonstrate that students can benefit from peer assessment through learning their own weaknesses in writing and leveraging received peer feedback to improve their writing performance. Meanwhile, they can gain considerably in terms of learning autonomy, critical reflection, self-assessment, and other key abilities that develop as they participate in peer assessment. This review finds that the scholarship on peer assessment in writing has examined peer assessment as learning and provided persuasive evidence in support of the aforementioned argument despite the limited amount of research. To fully capture a picture of peer assessment as learning, we urge more investigations to examine students' experiences from the AaL perspective in diverse contexts.

5 Peer Assessment in the EAP/ESP Writing Context

Since the beginning of the twenty-first century there has been a shift of focus from summative assessment to formative assessment (Wiliam, 2006). Against this backdrop, an increasing body of EAP/ESP writing studies has come to investigate the use of formative feedback or explore the formative implications of traditional summative assessments. In other words, although summative evaluation methods were employed to evaluate writing accuracy and revision performance, researchers have attempted to involve students in the assessment process to increase their efforts, awareness of, and motivations to participate in these activities, or to facilitate their writing processes and revisions, as summative assessment may also have additional formative functions (Topping, 1998).

5.1 Peer Assessment of Learning

Peer assessment has been widely investigated in ESP contexts for summative assessments. The characteristics and user acceptance of peer ratings on L2 learners' writing were investigated by Saito and Fujita (2004). In their comparison between peer rating, teacher rating, and self-rating on sixty-one Japanese freshmen majoring in business management, they found a similarity between the scores of teacher ratings and peer ratings, indicating that the quality of peer summative assessment is not inferior to teachers' assessment. Meanwhile, the study also found that peer ratings had no negative influence on learners' attitudes toward peer assessment, implying that implementing peer rating for evaluating learners' writing was feasible.

Some researchers have also examined summative peer assessment activities like requiring the participants to mark or grade their peers' writing based on given assessment rubrics or criteria for a formative purpose (Geithner & Pollastro, 2016). Among the studies that involve peer marking or grading on the assessment of peers' writing, rubrics and assessment criteria or pre-training were first presented for assessors to standardize their scores. In addition, they participated in relevant assessment training under the monitoring or assistance of teachers or certain staff. Both assessors and assessees acknowledged that they experienced learning gains in the process of providing summative assessment to their peers. In this sense, summative peer assessment could also serve a formative function rather than only being able to "judge learning from certification" (Lam, 2016, p. 1900). Under such circumstances, students might benefit from exposure to rubrics, checklists for the assessment process, discussion guidelines, and teachers or experts' assessment scaffolding through examining others' problems or comparing their own writing with that of their peers (Chang, 2016; Venables & Summit, 2003). Hence, they will be able to enhance their writing skills and accuracy, their understanding of subject-related knowledge, and their ability to analyze literature, as well as critically identifying problems (Geithner & Pollastro, 2016; Venables & Summit, 2003). To sum up, although conducted in a summative way, assessment in the form of scores and grades may still function in a formative way, contributing to both assessors and assessees' learning investment and gains, subject knowledge, and writing skills (Geithner & Pollastro, 2016; Saito & Fujita, 2004; Venables & Summit, 2003) in the ESP context.

The research on peer assessment for summative purposes in L2 writing in recent years has shown a decrease in the EAP writing context, as research has increasingly revealed the benefits of formative assessment practices in boosting learners' learning gains (Black and Wiliam, 1998). Under such circumstances, researchers have started to shift their attention to exploring the effects of formative assessment or a combination of both summative and formative feedback together on learners' learning gains in their writing and language achievement (Kumar & Stracke, 2011). This is due to the reason that summative feedback alone is less likely to substantially promote students' writing and language development, reduce knowledge gaps, and help both master's and PhD students find a place in the scholarly community. However, comparative studies exist that have explored different characteristics and the effects of summative assessment, including teacher-, peer-, and self-assessment on students' writing. For instance, Esfandiari and Myford (2013) employed a six-point Likert rating scale based on fifteen assessment criteria to assess the rigor of the assessment from different sources: teachers, peers, and the students themselves. It was found that teacher assessment was the most stringent, while self-assessment was the most lenient. This phenomenon was attributed to sociocultural factors, whereby Iranian students who did not "share the culture of modesty" (p. 125) might give themselves higher scores. Suggestions were made by the researchers to teachers to train students on how to assess based on given criteria or to work with other students to design the evaluation criteria so that they could strengthen their understanding of rubrics and hence evaluate in a more objective manner. In conclusion, unlike the studies in the ESP context, peer assessment research in the EAP context has tended to explore the formative function of peer assessment in promoting learners' language and skills development.

5.2 Peer Assessment for Learning

Based on the review, it is evident that the majority of studies on peer assessment have investigated the effects of peer assessment on students' writing or language development, as well as exploring how teachers could implement or design appropriate peer assessment activities (i.e., Chen, 2010; Venables & Summit, 2003; Yu & Lee, 2014; Yu et al., 2019). In studies in the EAP and ESP writing context, peer assessment was conducted both in and out of the classroom by providing comments on peers' drafts or work, including PhD and master's students. Apart from the common peer feedback forms or checklists, thesis writing groups were also commonly used to send and receive peer feedback via group interactions and communications (e.g., Chen, 2010; Man et al., 2018; Venables & Summit, 2003; Woodhouse & Wood, 2022; Yu, 2019; Yu et al., 2019; Zhang et al., 2022). Whatever the methods used to provide and receive peer assessment on writing, learners were found to improve their writing accuracy and skills, acquire subject knowledge, enhance their critical reading and writing skills, and strengthen their writing confidence and motivation, to name a few (Esfandiari & Myford, 2013; Ferguson, 2009; Venables & Summit, 2003; Wichmann et al., 2018). This shows that peer assessment can benefit students' writing, providing evidence for an AfL orientation in L2 writing literature in recent decades.

Most peer assessment studies in the ESP context aim at implementing this form of assessment so that learners can not only improve their writing accuracy or ability but also make progress in their subject knowledge, pre-service experience, sense of audience, critical thinking ability, writing confidence, and motivation through their revisions and error corrections, peer interactions and communications, and comparisons between their essays and those of their peers (Ferguson, 2009; McIsaac & Sepe, 1996; Thouesny & Bradley, 2014; Venables & Summit, 2003; Warschauer & Grimes, 2007). In a study conducted by Warschauer and Grimes (2007), Swedish computer engineering students were found to benefit from collaborative learning with their peers in a web-based environment like Google Drive. Their results indicate that such peer response activity contributes to learners' text development through gaining an insight into their drafts in the partner-engaged writing process and their joint construction of meanings. Peer interactions can be seen as an effective intervention to provide either implicit or explicit information for learners' development (Thouesny & Bradley, 2014). Apart from supporting learners in terms of error correction and writing revision, peer assessment in an ESP context was also also found to offer pre-service accountants valuable pre-professional experience and enhance their sense of audience, which could guide them in making decisions on textual organization, required information, specificity level, and appropriate tone while writing (McIsaac & Sepe, 1996). Furthermore, working with peers could also provide learners with emotional encouragement to write (Ferguson, 2009), and increase learners' time investment and efforts in revision and writing. Peer assessment was sometimes found to be more detailed than that of staff, indicating that peers took the task seriously (Venables & Summit, 2003).

In the ESP context, pedagogical implications can be drawn from the abovementioned studies. Teachers must play a role in instructing or monitoring peer assessment activities through pre-training and the provision of guidelines and criteria to avoid uncontrolled and superficial peer assessment. They should also facilitate peer discussions and involvement in topics (McIsaac & Sepe, 1996). Teachers could even give feedback on peer feedback to inform students of their problems in peer assessment, guiding them in how to provide constructive critiques and improve their feedback quality (Geithner & Pollastro, 2016).

Overall, the past decades have witnessed ample empirical evidence on the facilitating effects of peer assessment on students' writing learning and development in EAP contexts from different perspectives (e.g., Bhowmik et al., 2019; Ciampa & Wolfe, 2023; Esfandiari & Myford, 2013; Topping et al., 2000; Yu & Lee, 2014; Zou et al., 2018; Zhang et al., 2022). Research has shown that peer assessment can provide student authors with significant learning benefits, such as raising reader awareness and recommendations for further revision. Participants enrolled in a peer collaborative EAP course in the Canadian context in a study conducted by Bhowmik and colleagues (2019) shared that with immediate feedback from peers, they were informed of alternative ways of adjusting their text and learned different perspectives. Furthermore, in a study conducted by Ciampa and Wolfe (2023), doctoral students admitted the various benefits of peer review on improving their thesis proposals. Receiving feedback from peers can help improve the proposal clarity and offer insights into identifying gaps and expressing information. Similarly, Zhang and colleagues (2022) found that the doctoral students in their study acknowledged the effect of online peer feedback on helping with their revision and writing improvement. This is evidence of peer assessment for learning, as students' doctoral thesis proposals indeed benefited from receiving peer feedback.

Studies that compared peer assessment with staff or teacher assessment also identified desirable effects of peer assessment on learners' social and writing performance. For instance, Topping and colleagues (2000) found that through the repeated practices of reading and evaluating drafts based on assessment rubrics, learners could reduce their social-emotional discomfort when participating in the activities. Significance hence has been attached to peer comments for the sake of providing new information, increasing understanding of the pros and cons of writing, improving writing accuracy and performance, raising reader and writer awareness, and developing critical stances. Another comparative study by Esfandiari and Myford (2013) found peer assessment to have positive effects on learners' writing performance, attitude enhancement, self-esteem cultivation, along with positive communication.

Apart from the comparative studies mentioned in this section, teacher-supported peer feedback activities also have proved beneficial to students' language and writing development. Wichmann and colleagues (2018) examined the effects of sense-making support in the process of implementing peer assessment of academic writing activities at a German university. It was found that participants who received the teacher's sense-making support made fewer errors with increased revision accuracy. However, although their ability to label problems developed, their problem detection ability was not very satisfactory. The type, content, and delivery of feedback itself can partially explain this. It seemed that direct feedback was less likely to stimulate learners' motivation for problem detection, indicating that less cognitive effort had been devoted to the process (Wichmann et al., 2018). As a matter of fact, students' attitudes toward peer assessment were also related to their participation. In Zou and colleagues' (2018) study about the relationships among student attitudes, gender, distribution, and their participation in peer assessment, positive attitudes were found to negatively predict students' participation in the subsequent assessment practices. This could be explained by the fact that a longer comment in peer feedback requires more effort, and thus participants gradually became tired of participating in the activity.

Teachers and experts could learn from peer assessment activities to take learners' individual factors, including students' language proficiency, motivations and beliefs, and confidence, to name just a few, into consideration. This might have either a positive or negative influence on the quality and accuracy of peer assessment, as well as students' investment in it (Allen & Katayama, 2016; Esfandiari & Myford, 2013; Topping et al., 2000; Wichmann et al., 2018;). Meanwhile, they could provide training on how to engage students in peer feedback affectively, cognitively, and behaviorally. More specifically, apart from providing instruction on how to give feedback and how to revise their drafts, teachers could also consider developing students' self-confidence in giving and receiving feedback constantly, providing guidelines or criteria, designing appropriate activities and, when necessary, incorporating compulsory regulations to incentivize participation.

A variety of studies have shown that peer assessment activities can enhance postgraduate students' abilities to critically read and comprehend literature, provide peer comments, incorporate feedback into their writing, and find a place in the academic community (Geithner & Pollastro, 2016; Man et al., 2018; Yu et al., 2019). The benefits of peer assessment on postgraduate students' academic writing practices are also supported by studies that compared supervisory or other research staff assessment and peer assessment. For example, in Chen's (2010) study that compared peer and staff assessment, ten Taiwanese master's students reported a positive appraisal of the quality of peer comments on language, content, and organization problems compared with staff's comments on a surface level. They held positive attitudes toward their peer reviewing experience, expressing their appreciation for the constructive feedback they received that could help them discover the problems in their writing. Meanwhile, they were also afforded opportunities to reflect upon their own writing as assessors and were more critical when examining the accuracy of comments through self-checking. Caffarella and Barnett (2010), in another comparative study, investigated the importance of giving and receiving critiques for PhD students in a scholarly writing project The participants in their study regarded peer assessment as the most important driving force to promote their understanding of the scholarly writing process and their written performance. In other words, PhD students learned more about the academic writing process under the intervention of the scholarly writing project and hence found different ways to improve their drafts. Thanks to the personalized and iterative face-to-face peer feedback they received, students were provided opportunities to gain new information about a topic in the reading-and-assessing process as feedback givers. They compared their own drafts with their peers to reflect upon their drafts, thus contributing to improving their writing accuracy and other abilities.

Nonetheless, the positive effects of peer assessment on students' writing improvement are not without conditions. Yu and colleagues (2019) examined three master's students' affective, cognitive, and behavioral engagement with peer feedback on their thesis. Although the quality of their peer feedback was enhanced, participants' engagement with peer assessment was not satisfactory. The results demonstrated that students' emotions influenced their behavioral and cognitive efforts, leading to a less strategic revision of their drafts. Meanwhile, their participants acted as passive feedback receivers in order to be less cognitively overloaded. In such instances, peer feedback may not realize its maximum learning potential in developing master's students' academic writing ability or guiding them into the academic community (Yu & Lee, 2016b). In other words, learners with a low level of meaningful engagement with peer feedback affectively, cognitively and behaviorally may not improve their academic writing accuracy or enrich their subject or genre knowledge.

The abovementioned studies on peer assessment also provide enlightening implications for teachers and supervisors. In supervising or teaching scholarly writing, instead of incorporating peer feedback just as a classroom routine, instructors should be clear about the goals and benefits of the peer feedback process, try to assist learners in understanding how to receive and give effective feedback and how to reconcile conflicting feedback, acknowledge novice scholars' positive and negative emotions as reasonable reactions, provide training to assessors and assessees with clear guidelines and, when necessary, provide feedback on peer assessment (Caffarella & Barnett, 2010; Chen, 2010; Geithner & Pollastro, 2016; Yu et al., 2019).

5.3 Peer Assessment as Learning

Although there has been a comparatively lower number of studies with an orientation toward peer assessment as learning compared to studies that focused on peer assessment of learning and for learning, positive evidence regarding peer assessment as learning can still be gleaned from the extant literature (e.g., Ciampa & Wolfe, 2023; Gao et al., 2017; Huisman et al., 2018; Woodhouse & Wood, 2022; Yu, 2019). Research has shown that either as feedback givers or feedback receivers, learners can reap benefits from the assessment process and revision activities as well as the concomitant peer communications and interactions. These can contribute to improving their critical thinking or higher-order abilities, fostering self-reflection on their writing, and so on (Gao et al., 2017; Huisman et al., 2018; Topping et al., 2000). The findings of these studies shed some light on the significance of peer assessment in enabling learners to develop their cognitive and metacognitive capacities in self-evaluating their writing in both ESP and EAP contexts.

In the study conducted by Gao and colleagues (2017), the term "critical peer feedback" was proposed to describe an "integration of critical thinking and feedback" (p. 40). More specifically, critical peer feedback refers to "a kind of higher-order assessment of writing with the critical thinking skills of analysis, evaluation, and creation of peers' work by the cognition foundation of writing knowledge, writing task comprehension, and their application, which aims to scaffold peers' writing and at the same time construct self-cognition of writing ability" (p. 41). The qualitative study mainly investigated how critical peer feedback operated in students' business English writing. It was found that through the intervention of critical peer feedback activities, participants began to acquire knowledge of how to provide higher-order feedback beyond merely correcting form-focused errors. They showed desirable improvements in their feedback and writing quality, as well as emphasizing the ability to "create" and think critically both in their writing process and in their assessing process. Participants also agreed that their improved higher-order thinking skills to analyze, evaluate, and create in business English writing were considerably enhanced by examining their peers' writing under the guidance of teachers (Gao et al., 2017).

Previous studies have provided empirical evidence showing the benefits that both givers and receivers can gain in the process of peer feedback. The study by Huisman and colleagues (2018) tried to compare the respective effects of providing feedback and receiving feedback on learners' subsequent writing performance. Their findings suggested both activities had a similar impact, indicating that participating in peer feedback, either as feedback givers or receivers, offers an equal opportunity of improving learning. When responding to the feedback received, the participants of the study tended to focus more on exploratory feedback, as this kind of feedback required mindful cognitive operations and critical reflections on the students' own work, indicating that students can acquire a self-evaluative ability in the process of peer assessment (Huisman et al., 2018). These findings echoed the findings of Topping and colleagues (2000), who examined the reliability and validity of formative peer assessment in academic writing. In their study, participants reported peer assessment as not only a source of learning gains, but also as an effective way to help them reflect upon and improve their writing from a more critical stance. Furthermore, acting as assessors helped them cultivate transferable interpersonal and professional skills that can be applied to their future writing, indicating that peer assessment can be a suitable channel for fostering students' self-assessment abilities (Topping et al., 2000). These research findings all show that students can reap various benefits from participating in the peer assessment activity, such as improved critical reflection on their writing and self-evaluation or assessment abilities.

Specific positive evidence on the potential of peer assessment as a learning opportunity and its benefits can be found in EAP studies focused on postgraduate students. For example, the doctoral students in the study of Woodhouse and Wood (2022) indicated that participating in peer review made them more critically aware of and reflective of their own writing so as to improve their academic writing. Similarly, in the study of Ciampa and Wolfe (2023), the doctoral students admitted the various benefits of peer review on improving their thesis proposals. In addition to peers identifying problems in their writing, reviewing peers' work also made these students more critical and reflective of their own writing and even research problems. The experience of reviewing peers' writing motivated those doctoral students to examine their own writing to see whether similar problems existed in it, as well as facilitating their subsequent revision. This indicates that peer assessment was implemented as learning. Situating peer assessment in a postgraduate thesis writing context, Yu (2019) revealed a variety of learning benefits from postgraduate students giving peer feedback on their master's thesis writing. Students reported learning about the structure and components of postgraduate theses from reading peers' work. In addition, the identification of problems in peers' writing served to remind the students to monitor their own writing process to avoid similar problems. In the case of issues of uncertainty, the peer feedback giver was even promoted to recruit external resources to check for these potential errors before giving feedback. This indicates that students reaped learning benefits while they were experiencing peer feedback, providing rich support to peer assessment as learning.

Considering the fact that postgraduate students are usually required to write by synthesizing sources, using different strategies to realize knowledge transformation and construction within certain academic communities, Yang (2016) employed a computer-supported collaborative learning system to explore how postgraduate students benefit from peer feedback in knowledge transformation and construction when involved in summary writing. The findings revealed that participants were able to transform their knowledge by clarifying syntactic and textual problems in peer feedback, and at the same time their reading and academic writing ability also improved. Furthermore, through giving and receiving feedback, students not only raised their language awareness but also enhanced their critical thinking skills by not only pointing out other's issues but also reflecting on their own writing.

6 Peer Assessment in the ESL/EFL School Writing Context

In general, very few empirical studies have been conducted on the role and functions of peer assessment in ESL/EFL school writing contexts. In this section, I draw upon the limited research in school writing contexts to analyze how peer assessment can work as summative and formative instruments and tools in evaluating and improving primary and secondary students' writing quality.

6.1 Peer Assessment of Learning

Overall, there has been little empirical research focusing on peer summative assessment of L2 writing conducted in non-tertiary school contexts. Schunn and colleagues (2016) explored whether high school students can assess their peers writing accurately based on a designed assessment rubric in the United States. The researchers compared the students' peer ratings and feedback given on *Peercept*, a web-based system, with both their teachers' and expert scorers' assessments of the same writing. The results indicated that through implementing a well-designed rubric, high school students had the ability to provide more valid ratings than a single teacher, and their ratings proved to be as valid as those given by professional scorers. To compare the effectiveness of peer assessment and teacher feedback, Tsagari and Meletiadou (2015) adopted a quasi-experimental design to divide sixty intermediate-level Cypriot adolescent (thirteen or fourteen-year-old) EFL learners into three mixed-ability groups: Group A (receiving teacher feedback), Group B (receiving teacher feedback and peer feedback), and Group C (receiving teacher feedback and giving peer feedback). The experiment results indicated that the experimental groups not only provided reliable summative assessment (i.e., similar marks to their teachers'), but they also gained a clear understanding of the particular assessment standard.

In previous empirical research, although peer feedback was not investigated as a summative tool that directly assesses students' writing performance or ability, its reliability and validity were tested and its value has been recognized by both teachers and students in various L1 and L2 contexts. The studies mentioned earlier in this section made several recommendations for summative assessment, including creating a task-specific rubric to facilitate students' fair peer assessment (Schunn et al., 2016) and training young learners to provide peer feedback as well as scaffolding them to conduct this assessment process (Peterson & McClay, 2010). However, Double and his coauthors (2020) conducted a meta-analysis to investigate the crucial role of peer grading in determining the effectiveness of peer feedback. Their findings revealed that peer grading was advantageous for tertiary students but did not yield the same benefits for primary or secondary school students. They suggested that peer grading, as a form of summative evaluation, appeared to make a limited contribution to the peer feedback process among non-tertiary students. Similar to the higher education context, the positive effect on using anonymity during peer assessment among school students remains unclear since it does not necessarily result in a higher grade or function as a symbol of competitiveness, as is the case in higher education (Panadero & Alqassab, 2019).

6.2 Peer Assessment for Learning

The majority of empirical studies have concentrated on exploring the effectiveness of peer assessment or feedback on improving both primary and secondary students' writing performance, as well as teachers' awareness and instructions. Several studies have compared the acceptance of peer feedback and teacher feedback on writing (Lee, 2015; Tsagari & Meletiadou, 2015; Tsui & Ng, 2000) and investigated the correlation between students' writing ability and their peer feedback quality (Chong, 2018). Others have shed light on the interactions between peer feedback givers and receivers to investigate how peer assessment and its training improve students' writing performance (Peterson & Portier, 2014; Almahasneh & Abdul-Hamid, 2019; Tsagari & Meletiadou, 2015; Tsui & Ng, 2000), especially on how peer feedback could benefit feedback givers' writing performance (Berggren, 2015, 2019; Crinon, 2012; Lee, 2015). Moreover, other studies focused on teachers' perceptions and actions when implementing peer feedback in writing classrooms (Boon, 2016; Meletiadou, 2021a), as well as the integration of technology or the online context in peer feedback activities (Amalia, 2021; Nicolaidou, 2013; Vorobel, 2013; Woo et al., 2013).

6.2.1 Peer Assessment in the Secondary School Writing Context

To compare the effectiveness of peer feedback and teacher feedback in a secondary EFL/ESL writing context, Tsui and Ng (2000) conducted a mixed-approach study on the roles of peer comments on writing revisions provided by senior secondary L2 learners (Grades 12 & 13) in Hong Kong. Though students viewed the teacher as "a figure of authority" (p. 147), the authors still identified four positive roles of peer comments from the interview data as "enhancing a sense of audience; awareness raising through reading peers' writing; encouraging collaborative learning and fostering ownership of text" (p. 147). Within the same context in Hong Kong, Lee (2015) conducted additional research on the effectiveness of different students' peer feedback stages on their ESL writing. Focusing on junior secondary students, Lee (2015) employed questionnaires and interviews to investigate participants' perspectives on two main peer feedback stages: traditional reviewer–writer exchanges and a newly proposed intra-feedback practice compared to teachers' feedback on writing. The findings echoed previous studies, showing that junior secondary ESL students also valued teacher feedback and urging the combination of teacher and peer feedback. Furthermore, the study emphasized the necessity of intra-feedback (i.e., an activity that involves peer feedback on peer feedback and is directed at reviewers) as a process for reviewers to provide peer feedback on their planned peer comments before meeting with the writers (receivers).

Noticing the benefits of peer assessment for writing learning, Almahasneh and Abdul-Hamid (2019) further examined the impact of peer assessment training on the writing performance of 120 Arab EFL secondary school students between the ages of fifteen and sixteen in Malaysia. According to the results of the pre-test and post-test on their writing performance, secondary EFL students who participated in peer assessment training produced writing drafts of a higher quality than those who only received conventional essay writing instructions from teachers without peer assessment training.

Under the perspective of AfL, peer feedback could also benefit feedback givers' writing performance. Berggren (2015, 2019) conducted two intervention studies to examine how Swedish junior EFL secondary students improved their writing performance through giving peer feedback. During the interventions, the students wrote two drafts in various genres (i.e., a reply letter, a newspaper article, and an argumentative essay), and the involved teachers jointly constructed criteria lists, provided feedback training, and conducted peer assessment in groups. The findings suggested that learning from giving feedback was operationalized to not only raise participants' awareness of the audience and genre, but also to stimulate feedback givers' further revisions and to transfer ideas as links between the revision or changes on the first drafts and their peer feedback provision.

Though peer assessment has been argued to be beneficial for students' writing performance, teachers' role in ensuring the effectiveness of peer assessment or feedback cannot be neglected. Lindgren (2018) suggested that Swedish secondary English teachers saw the necessity to conduct various peer review activities (e.g., oral or written) according to different writing projects or tasks. By implementing various peer review activities, they were able to improve students' critical thinking and use of English during peer discussion, thereby improving their writing in the process. Furthermore, with adequate teacher instruction and training, students can familiarize themselves with the assessment standards or rubrics, and peer assessment can be successfully applied to support the integration of instruction with AfL enhancement and progress (Meletiadou, 2021a).

In short, peer assessment (or feedback) was valued by most students and teachers with different abilities and backgrounds in studies conducted in secondary school contexts. Improvements in the language proficiency, writing ability, and skills of ESL/EFL students, along with critical thinking in L2 writing with knowledge of its assessment criteria, were believed to have resulted from teachers' comprehensive instructions, well-designed assessment standards or rubrics, and sufficient scaffolding throughout the whole peer assessment process.

6.2.2 Peer Assessment in the Primary School Writing Context

In the primary school context, previous research has investigated the effectiveness of peer feedback from the teachers' perspective (Boon, 2016), as well as the interactions between feedback givers and receivers (Crinon, 2012; Peterson & Portier, 2014). Boon (2016) conducted action research to increase British primary Grade 6 students' uptake of peer feedback during their peer assessment of writing. As both the researcher and teacher, the researcher took measures to guide students on effective peer feedback strategies, provide enough time for revision and discussion and, finally, provide a simple response sheet for the students to understand how to modify and improve their writing pieces based on such peer feedback. The results suggested that for young learners to make effective use of peer assessment on writing, their feedback needs to be task involving and practical. Moreover, other strategies should be implemented by teachers, such as providing time for their actual revisions, discussion with peers for clarifying misunderstandings, and reflection on the improvement of writing quality.

Studies have found peer feedback interactions among primary writers to be spontaneous, though with teachers' guidance during their instructions. Peterson and Portier (2014) conducted a longitudinal field observation in a Canadian Grade 1 ESL classroom. Under the modeling of the teacher, young ESL learners could follow the sample effective feedback to provide more content-oriented feedback than convention-oriented ones, which they embedded in their spontaneous talk during the writing process. In contrast to the findings of Chong (2018), which suggested a positive relationship between secondary students' writing ability and the quality of their provided feedback, the Grade 1 students with different levels of language ability were equally willing to provide feedback on peers' pictures and content of writing. It was notable that more advanced students were able to imitate the teacher's criterion-based feedback during this process. Meanwhile, echoing the findings from the secondary school context, primary school students have also been found to benefit from the process of providing feedback. For instance, Crinon (2012) used email corres-pondence to teach narrative writing skills to primary Grade 4 and 5 students in Paris. This study uncovered that through peer feedback revision processes, participants increased their understanding of the narrative genre and its key features; thus, they improved the quality of their revised texts, especially among those who were peer feedback givers.

Another line of research examined how to enhance the learning of writing skills in both elementary and secondary contexts by incorporating technology into peer assessment. With the assistance of various technological tools, such as Wikis (Woo et al., 2013) and e-portfolios (Nicolaidou, 2013), peer assessment was found to have a positive effect on primary students' provision of peer feedback, especially on more macro-level feedback (i.e., content) and corrective feedback than micro-level or surface-level changes. For secondary EFL stu-dents, Franco Ponce and his coauthors (2021) applied ICT tools (i.e., Google Docs, Live worksheet, and Padlet) in training participants in peer review. The results uncovered that not only did their writing grades improve but also their writing and peer feedback skills, which aligned with the findings in the primary context (Nicolaidou, 2013). However, such ICT-integrated training practices could not replace the teacher's role in the writing classroom (Franco Ponce et al., 2021).

To integrate technology into students' peer assessment, teachers have to take responsibility for explicitly providing instruction in both writing and using technological tools (Amalia, 2021). Moreover, they need to encourage revision-oriented peer feedback and scaffold students to enhance the effectiveness of their peer feedback. When using Wikis, teachers could demonstrate how to provide timely feedback and explain what kinds of revision-oriented feedback should be provided (Woo et al., 2013). In the e-portfolio case, teachers could give sample feedback on students' portfolios and give them enough time to try using a designed feedback code sheet (Nicolaidou, 2013). However, Amalia (2021) critiqued teachers remaining at the center of explaining the definitions and benefits of peer assessment for students instead of training students in how to conduct peer assessment, including detailed criteria and description of the rubric. In such a teacher-centered scenario, students lacked discussion with their peers, instead merely following the soft copy of the rubric sent by the teacher. Therefore, under the perspective of peer assessment for learning, teachers need to provide more detailed and practical scaffolding for students' peer assessment, with enough time, prepared materials (i.e., rubrics with explanations), and guidance to enhance their writing learning as a process that includes writing, discussion, and revision.

6.3 Peer Assessment as Learning

Little research has investigated how peer assessment plays an AaL role, which enables students to develop their cognitive and metacognitive capacity or use peer assessment as an independent self-evaluation of their writing ability (Bui & Kong, 2019; Harris et al., 2015; Lee et al., 2019). Although the previous findings did not directly emphasize peer assessment as a method of self-evaluation, they still provided some insights into students' learner autonomy and self-reflection on understanding and internalizing the given assessment rubrics to evaluate and improve their own writing (Amalia, 2021; Meletiadou, 2021b; Tsagari & Meletiadou, 2015). Some empirical evidence has supported the idea that students' critical thinking abilities could be developed within peer assessment by reviewing their peers' texts as a reader and deciding how to apply the feedback they receive during the revision process (Berggren, 2015; Lindgren, 2018; Ruegg, 2015; Tsui & Ng, 2000).

From the perspective of teachers, students could be trained to develop themselves as writing learning resources, increase their writing motivation, and utilize metacognition to improve the quality of peer review. Lee and her coauthors (2019) uncovered that through training primary students on how to conduct peer assessment using criteria for effective peer comments, they could become their own and each other's writing learning resources. Meanwhile, the implementation of peer assessment was found to reduce primary students' writing anxiety and increase their writing motivation (Tunagür, 2021). Aside from teaching primary students how to provide useful peer feedback as learning resources, metacognitive training on peer review could increase secondary students' amount of content-related feedback and help them engage and collaborate more during peer review tasks on L2 writing; this should be particularly considered seriously when it comes to incorporating peer feedback during revision (Bui & Kong, 2019). However, there is little evidence of self-regulated feedback in primary and secondary students' peer assessment on writing. Harris and colleagues (2015) argued that this could be attributed to students' heavy cognitive burden expended on identifying problems along with solutions, concerns about interpersonal relationships, and teachers' constrained feedback practices that neglected the self-regulation aspect of peer assessment in writing.

To summarize, there is no unified conclusion on the role of peer assessment in developing students' cognitive and metacognitive capacities in self-evaluating their writing ability due to the limited scholarly attention given to the AaL perspective of peer assessment in writing. Scholars, however, have called for more research into how to use peer assessment to encourage learner-centered assessment and develop critical thinking skills for lifelong learning (Harris et al., 2015; Lee, 2017; Lee et al., 2019).

7 Peer Assessment in Foreign Language Writing Contexts

As peer assessment has shown its great potential to improve students' learning outcomes, a growing number of researchers have tried to investigate how peer feedback works in different contexts. In recent years, a growing number of studies have examined peer feedback/assessment in languages other than English writing contexts. This section, guided by the conceptual framework of "peer assessment of/for/as learning," aims to depict the landscape of peer feedback in foreign language learning contexts in terms of what learners can obtain from peer assessment in foreign language writing and through examining the orientations in the extant literature toward peer assessment in foreign language writing.

7.1 Peer Assessment of Learning

Careful examination of the extant literature showed that most studies in foreign language writing contexts had a formative assessment focus when investigating peer assessment, with insufficient evidence from a few studies to elucidate the equivalence of peer assessment and teacher assessment as summative tools. Though scholars have appealed for peer feedback training on improving writing and its revision quality (Min, 2018; Zhang & Yu, 2022), a study by Altstaedter (2018) found that despite differences in the focus of feedback, there was no significant difference in terms of increased writing quality between the trained and untrained groups. The researcher, therefore, argued that while the effectiveness of peer assessment in improving students' writing has been proven primarily in EFL contexts, it is not guaranteed to have an impact in other foreign language learning contexts.

7.2 Peer Assessment for Learning

Overall, it is clear from the examination of earlier studies that peer assessment has mostly been used in foreign language learning contexts from the standpoint of AfL. In other words, there exists a preponderance of studies devoted to examining the effects of peer assessment on students' foreign language writing development, providing an abundance of supportive evidence regarding the benefits of peer assessment for learning. Specifically, previous research has elaborated on the detailed processes and mechanisms regarding how students learn from peer assessment, that is, how peer assessment for learning manifests itself in different contexts. Peer feedback/revision involved in collaborative learning can greatly improve students' writing performance in various ways. As Tian (2011) has claimed, collaborative writing has the potential to improve the quality of students' Chinese L2 writing by giving them the opportunity to scaffold each other, to correct each other's errors, and to combine their strengths in the target language. Later, Strobl (2014) added further evidence by showing that in-depth discussion during the planning phase contributed to higher scores in German L2 collaborative writing performance. When students were engaged in collaborative writing, the negotiation process offered them a good opportunity to slow down their writing pace, facilitating better writing performance in German. This could be due to the fact that by meeting with fellow students, students slow down their writing process, which helps them reflect on the ideas in their writing and ultimately improves the depth and meaningfulness of their writing (Snyder et al., 2016). On the other hand, peer review activity allows reviewers an opportunity to perfect their own writing. As O'Donnell (2014) has stated, after reading peers' writing, students may learn additional ideas to enrich their own writing. This is also corroborated by Yu and Lee's study (2016b) where through peer review, the reviewers were able to raise their awareness of audience and genre, simulate further revisions, as well as improve their writing abilities at the global level.

Apart from the abovementioned learning affordances of peer assessment, students can increase their reader awareness, engage in meaning negotiation, as well as provide scaffolding and social support (Altstaedter, 2018; Bueno-Alastuey et al., 2022; Illana-Mahiques, 2021; McDonough et al., 2021, 2022; Sánchez-Naranjo, 2019). Although the conducted studies may have had different foci in their investigation of peer assessment, including the role of peer review training, peer reviewer or giver, and peer assessment at different stages of foreign language writing, they all provided empirical evidence about how peer assessment promotes students' writing learning and development. Situated in a Spanish as a foreign language course at an American university, Altstaedter (2018) found that either the treatment group receiving peer feedback training or the control group that had not received training made significant improvements in writing quality after participating in peer feedback. Similarly, Sánchez-Naranjo (2019) examined the effect of trained peer review on L2 Spanish learners' writing quality, finding that the trained peer review group had made more gains than the control group in the final versions of the text with revisions. McDonough and colleagues (2021) examined the relationship between L2 French learners' perceptions of peer interaction and their conversational patterns in interactive writing classes that involved peer interactions in the planning, revision, and the whole collaborative writing process. They found that students with more positive perceptions tended to initiate more conversations on language issues in their writing assignments. The case of one student being able to correct linguistic errors due to his partners' suggestions in the interactive revision phase shows an AfL orientation and provides supportive evidence regarding the AfL effects of peer assessment. These studies, despite the differences in focus, also examined the effects of peer review on students' foreign writing performance and quality, constituting an AfL orientation. And the research findings, indeed, lend empirical support to peer assessment's potential for improving students' foreign language learning.

Nonetheless, not all participants in peer assessment may have equal access to this learning potential. Illana-Mahiques (2021) examined the role of the peer feedback receiver or giver in the quality of L2 Spanish learners' final writing, finding that the amount of feedback given by feedback givers can significantly predict their writing quality. This finding provides empirical evidence for the learning benefits of reviewing and was interpreted in relation to the possibility that reviewers can learn from reviewing peers' writing to critically assess, revise, and improve their own writing. In addition to the differential learning potential of peer assessment for reviewers and receivers, the sequence or stage of peer review in the whole writing process was also found to be a significant factor. McDonough and colleagues (2022) investigated the effects of peer interactions before and after writing stages on the quality of L2 French learners' writing, finding that the group with pre-writing discussions had better performance in grammar and lexis, whereas the group with peer revision failed to demonstrate improvements. However, Bueno-Alastuey and colleagues (2022) focused on comparing the effect of collaborative writing and peer feedback under different sequences on students' writing quality in a Spanish as foreign language context. Under either condition, students showed improvements, providing evidence for peer feedback as AfL, particularly for language improvement such as in syntactic complexity and fluency. These conflicting findings could be due to the different contexts and different measurements of writing improvement. Further investigations on peer assessment for learning in foreign languages other than English writing contexts can contribute a more refined understanding of such differential learning potential.

In addition, positive evidence on the use of peer assessment for learning can also be found in studies situated in synchronous and asynchronous writing environments as well as cross-cultural writing contexts. Students usually provide their peers with cognitive and social acknowledgment, and the students who gave the most social and cognitive acknowledgment were also those who contributed most to the feedback activity, even though their language competence was not as advanced as expected (Heift & Caws, 2000). Regarding cross-cultural email exchange, Jogan and colleagues (2001) found that this kind of exchange improves students' knowledge about and commitment to the target culture as students can cross boundaries to more easily build empathy in order to lay the foundation for more in-depth cultural understanding. Another interesting point in their study is the idea that this kind of asynchronous communication with a native speaker from the target culture might offer a comforting environment for the nonnative speaker in the sense that students are able to control the development of their dialogue, which otherwise would be unlikely to happen in traditional classrooms.

In a study of computer-mediated peer responses in a college Spanish classroom, Roux-Rodriguez (2003) investigated students' responses to peer feedback. The results indicated that students regarded their peers' feedback as a content resource for their writing or used their peers' feedback to polish their writing language. In this context, peer revision also proceeded more quickly as students could look up vocabulary rather than rely on synchronous negotiation of meaning to clarify unfamiliar items (Ware & O'Dowd, 2008). Moreover, Ruecker (2010) examined the learning potential of dual-language cross-cultural peer review between Chilean and US students and how it influences traditional monolingual and monocultural peer review, identifying several affective advantages of cross-cultural peer review that benefited both peer feedback givers and receivers. On the one hand, students were willing to accept and respond to feedback because they trusted feedback from more proficient peers; on the other hand, feedback givers who were placed in positions of authority felt more confident and inspired to give feedback because they believed their feedback would be useful to other language learners. Furthermore, participation in dual-language cross-cultural peer reviews boosted learners' confidence by providing a positive environment in which students could share their learning challenges (Ruecker, 2010). Certain social and cognitive skills of participants can be improved when peer feedback across different cultures is conducted in a telecollaborative manner (Lee, 2011), which confirms the viewpoint of Kinginger and Belz (2005) that learners in their study were aware of pragmatic issues because they frequently used politeness strategies to participate in feedback processes as a form of intercultural communication.

Furthermore, different types of peer feedback have varying degrees of influence on students' learning. For example, giving verbal peer feedback appears to promote students' overall English competence, as giving peer feedback is a complex linguistic and communicative activity that involves written and oral production, as well as listening, reading, speaking, and writing skills (Blain, 2001). Unmotivated learners may benefit from the peer learning activity as well, as they may feel encouraged to participate in a shared activity due to the influence of their more motivated peers. Learners tend to take more responsibility for their learning when engaging in peer interactions, attempting to provide more input and feedback that mediates learners' L2 development (Wu, 2009).

7.3 Peer Assessment as Learning

This review has found that the extant literature on peer assessment in writing is particularly concerned with the effects of peer assessment on learners' writing development in terms of better writing performance and higher writing or revision scores, which exactly coincides with the AfL orientation. Nonetheless, the past decades have also witnessed an increasing number of studies that have noticed the learning affordances of peer assessment as learning, despite constituting a relatively small portion of the studies on peer assessment in writing. And in some cases, the orientations of both AfL and AaL coexist. Through incorporating peer comments in revision, students are able to build up their learner autonomy, promote self-regulation, and develop social skills (Hu, 2005; Hyland & Hyland, 2006; Liu & Hansen Edwards, 2002).

Research has shown that students' learning autonomy, critical reflection, metacognitive awareness, and self-assessment can be fostered and boosted through peer assessment activities (López-Pellisa et al., 2020). For instance, the learning gains from peer assessment in relation to metacognitive and critical reflection are supported by the study conducted by López-Pellisa and colleagues (2020). Their study provided empirical evidence for peer feedback for AfI and AaL in a Spanish context, whereby students demonstrated improved writing proficiency and increased reflection on areas they can work on in their writing after engaging with peer feedback.

8 Moving Forward with Peer Assessment in Writing Instruction: Possibilities for Future Dialogue

This Element aims to provide a critical discussion of the major themes and research findings in existing studies on peer assessment with regard to the three assessment paradigms. It seeks to illustrate how peer assessment can play a role in the summative evaluation of students' writing ability, reveal how peer assessment can generate feedback for teachers to enhance their instruction and for students to improve their writing, and demonstrate how peer assessment enables students to develop their cognitive and metacognitive capacities in self-evaluating their writing ability in different sociocultural and educational contexts. While various aspects of peer assessment in different writing contexts have been investigated, the research scholarship seems to view peer assessment predominantly as a mechanism of AfL. There seems to be a habituated portrait of peer assessment as an AfL strategy through which learners use established criteria to tell each other what they have achieved and where improvement is needed. The analysis in the previous sections has confirmed that peer assessment can serve both summative and formative purposes in various writing instructional contexts, given the overlapping functions between AoL, AfL, and AaL. Specifically, peer assessment and grading have the potential to enable reliable and valid judgment and evaluation of peer writing, although firm causal evidence in some writing contexts, such as L2 school writing and foreign language writing contexts, needs to be provided in future research. Further empirical research can be conducted to further examine the measurement and evaluative functions of peer assessment and grading in writing instructions from the AoL perspective. We also need more knowledge regarding how peer grading leads to student learning in different writing contexts.

While research on peer assessment has proliferated in recent decades, more empirical studies in under-researched contexts such as non-English foreign language writing and school writing are required to gain a better understanding of how peer assessment can improve writing teaching and learning. More attention could be paid to young L2 writers and students learning to write in a foreign language. Most of the previous research has taken an AfL approach to peer assessment research in almost all the different writing contexts to reveal how peer assessment can benefit student writers in terms of text revisions, the improvement of writing quality, as well as writing development in the long run. This strand of studies has also examined how peer assessment activities in both traditional classroom and computer-mediated contexts can be appropriately implemented to improve student writing. A more AaL-oriented approach toward peer assessment is needed to investigate how participating in peer assessment activities in different writing contexts could empower students to be active and reflective writers who can evaluate their own weaknesses and strengths in different genres of writing, set up their own writing goals, and regulate and monitor their own writing progress through a range of scaffolding strategies.

To bridge the gap between research and practice in terms of implementing peer assessment in writing classrooms, it is suggested that researchers and practitioners take the research and instructional context into consideration when interpreting research findings. According to the existing literature, the effect of peer assessment on the development of both teachers and learners is still mixed and inconsistent, and this should be interpreted in light of individual and contextual factors. Positive effects such as improving learners' writing accuracy and ability, motivation and confidence in writing, and critical and transferable skills have been reported, while negative effects such as increasing students' social-academic discomfort and inducing frustrations have also been revealed. These occurrences could be attributed to a variety of individual and contextual factors. On the one hand, individual factors such as students' proficiency levels, previous feedback and writing experience, lower self-confidence in providing feedback, lower self-autonomy and motivation in practice, and personal negative emotions may influence the quality of comments, thereby limiting the effects of peer assessment in promoting writing and other self-regulated skills learning (e.g., Allen & Katayama, 2016; Caffarella & Barnett, 2000; Chen, 2010; Man et al., 2018; Venables & Summit, 2003; Yang, 2016; Yu et al., 2019; Zou et al., 2018). Contextual factors such as Confucius culture, institutional policies, teacher-centered teaching mode, lack of teacher scaffolding, insufficient supervision with simplified summative feedback, and inefficient peer communication can all impede student learning and writing development in peer assessment on a macro level (i.e., Esfandiari & Myford, 2013; Gao et al., 2017; Kumar & Stracke, 2011; Topping et al., 2000; Yu & Lee, 2014). These elements are intertwined and interact to influence the effectiveness of peer assessment.

While the literature has highlighted that peer assessment in various contexts can be an effective method *for* and *as* L2 writing learning, playing an important role in formative assessment and student-centered assessment processes, implementing peer assessment in L2 writing classrooms is not easy (Wanner & Palmer, 2018; Yu & Lee, 2016b). Its implementation and its role in assessment processes are subject to the influence of various individual and contextual factors. For instance, cultural issues, including students' cultural background, power distance, concern with "face," and assessment cultures, have been found to exert influence on L2 university students' participation in peer assessment activities (Allaei & Connor, 1990; Carson & Nelson, 1994; Hyland, 2000; Yu et al., 2016). Improper comments, unhelpful feedback, misunderstandings, and peer conflicts may arise in the L2 university context where students could have divergent conceptions due to cultural issues. Coupled with constraints of individual factors, such as student capacity and proficiency (e.g., Nguyen, 2008; Yu & Hu, 2017) and teacher involvement (e.g., Wanner & Palmer, 2018; Zhao, 2018), the implementation of peer assessment *for* and *as* learning remains challenging.

These findings point to the important role of writing teachers in implementing peer assessment in writing classrooms. As shown in the previous sections, writing teachers' scaffolding and peer assessment training are particularly important for primary and secondary school students in L2 writing contexts. While the published literature has shown that peer assessment and training are crucial to the effectiveness of this assessment strategy, more classroom-based qualitative research and action research could be conducted to examine how peer assessment is designed and implemented for AoL, AfL, and AaL purposes in specific writing instructional contexts. Another important area of research that can help close the research–practice gap is the impact of teacher education on teachers' assessment and feedback literacy when implementing peer assessment for various assessment and learning purposes. What can teachers of writing do to improve their assessment and feedback literacy? How do teacher education courses and teacher training programs influence writing teachers' understanding, use, and implementation of peer assessment to meet various assessment and learning goals in specific writing instructional contexts? What are the difficulties and challenges that writing teachers face when implementing peer assessment in writing classrooms to improve student learning? Addressing these questions can have beneficial pedagogical implications for teachers who want to learn how to use peer assessment as an important teaching and learning strategy and approach in their own classrooms.

To maximize the learning potential of peer assessment in writing classrooms, writing researchers and practitioners also need to enhance student engagement with peer assessment because the current research has highlighted the crucial roles of student writers' individual differences and agency in peer assessment activities. Researchers have paid increasing attention in recent years to studies of student engagement with peer assessment and written feedback from various perspectives, having recognized the importance of student engagement in their learning and academic success. Student engagement has been viewed as a meta-construct consisting of three components: affective/emotional, cognitive, and behavioral (Han & Hyland, 2015; Zhang & Hyland, 2018; Zhang, 2017; Zheng & Yu, 2018). Some early research on peer feedback engagement focused on the behavioral aspect, as evidenced by students' revision efforts in response to feedback and visible techniques for improving writing quality (Fan & Xu, 2020; Yu et al., 2019). Since it is argued that merely concentrating on the behavioral dimension is insufficient to comprehend the multifaceted nature of engagement with peer feedback because emotions and cognition are also crucial elements influencing L2 learning, recent research has also examined how students cognitively and affectively engaged with peer assessment (Fan & Xu, 2020; Yu et al., 2019). Fan and Xu (2020), for example, investigated the emotional, behavioral, and cognitive responses of twenty-one university EFL students to their engagement with form-focused and content-focused peer feedback in L2 writing. The results demonstrated that the sort of feedback affected how students engaged with it: Students experienced positive emotional engagement and substantial behavioral and cognitive engagement with the form-focused feedback, while with content-focused feedback they showed a low propensity for cognitive and behavioral engagement. Yu and colleagues (2019) further explored the inter-relation between the three subconstructs through a qualitative case study. The investigation of three master's students' engagement with peer feedback revealed that students' affective engagement could have positive or negative impacts on their behavioral and cognitive engagement. These findings can deepen our understanding of student participation in peer assessment activities. One important pedagogical implication is to encourage writing teachers to pay attention to different dimensions of student engagement in peer assessment activities, as well as to provide training to students regarding how to engage behaviorally, cognitively, and affectively with peer assessment.

To move forward with peer assessment in writing instruction, writing researchers also need to conduct research regarding how to develop student writing assessment and feedback literacy, which has been an emerging and important field of academic inquiry in recent years (Yu & Liu, 2021). Ever since its conception by Sutton in 2012, feedback literacy has drawn increasing scholarly attention and is now viewed as one of the core literacies that shape students' learning. It concerns learners' perceptions, evaluations, abilities, and emotion regulation in feedback situations, which disentangles the complexity of (non)learning from feedback and enables pedagogical interventions aiming for long-term improvement. To maximize student learning from peer assessment, growing emphasis should be placed on the student role in sense-making and using feedback and assessment for enhancement purposes (Mao & Lee, 2022, 2023). Student assessment and feedback literacy can be conceptualized as emerging, situated, and diversified literacy practices, identities, and cognitions. It concerns the way students perceive the value of assessment and feedback, understand the different affordances of different assessment and feedback sources, evaluate the usefulness of assessment and feedback, and manage emotions in peer assessment situations. This way of interpreting learning from feedback presents a dynamic, learner-centered view and necessitates a context-sensitive understanding of learners' thinking, being, and doing. Student assessment and feedback literacy also reflects students' adaptive literacy in peer assessment-related situations, and it is a repertoire of long-standing competencies. Future researchers need to draw scholarly and pedagogical attention to students' long-term development of assessment and feedback literacy in peer assessment activities for AoL, AfL, and AaL purposes and functions in various writing instructional contexts.

References

Ahmed, R., & Abdu, A. K. (2021). Online and face-to-face peer review in academic writing: Frequency and preferences. *Eurasian Journal of Applied Linguistics*, *7*(1), 169–201. https://doi.org/10.32601/ejal.911245.

Allaei, S. K., & Connor, U. (1990). Exploring the dynamics of cross-cultural collaboration in writing classrooms. *The Writing Instructor*, *10*(1), 19–28.

Allen, D., & Katayama, A. (2016). Relative second language proficiency and the giving and receiving of written peer feedback. *System*, *56*, 96–106. https://doi.org/10.1016/j.system.2015.12.002.

Almahasneh, A. M. S., & Abdul-Hamid, S. (2019). The effect of using peer assessment training on writing performance among Arab EFL high school students in Malaysia. *Arab World English Journal*, *10*(1), 105–115. https://dx.doi.org/10.24093/awej/vol10no1.10.

Althauser, R., & Darnall, K. (2001). Enhancing critical reading and writing through peer reviews: An exploration of assisted performance. *Teaching Sociology*, *29*(1), 23–35. https://doi.org/10.2307/1318780.

Altstaedter, L. (2018). Investigating the impact of peer feedback in foreign language writing. *Innovation in Language Learning and Teaching*, *12*(2), 137–151. https://doi.org/10.1080/17501229.2015.1115052.

Amalia, N. R. (2021). The implementation of peer assessment in online writing class at senior high school in Bawean. *Research on English Language Teaching in Indonesia*, *9*(1), 179–186.

Anson, I. G., & Anson, C. M. (2017). Assessing peer and instructor response to writing: A corpus analysis from an expert survey. *Assessing Writing*, *33*, 12–24. https://doi.org/10.1016/j.asw.2017.03.001.

Baker, K. M. (2016). Peer review as a strategy for improving students' writing process. *Active Learning in Higher Education*, *17*(3), 179–192. https://doi.org/10.1177/1469787416654794.

Barkaoui, K. (2021). *Evaluating tests of second language development*. Peter Lang.

Bauer, C., Figl, K., Derntl, M., Beran, P. P., & Kabicher, S. (2009). The student view on online peer reviews. *SIGCSE Bulletin*, *41*(3), 26–30. https://doi.org/10.1145/1562877.1562892.

Becker, A. (2016). Student-generated scoring rubrics: Examining their formative value for improving ESL students' writing performance. *Assessing Writing*, *29*, 15–24. https://doi.org/10.1016/j.asw.2016.05.002.

Berggren, J. (2015). Learning from giving feedback: A study of secondary-level students. *ELT Journal, 69*(1), 58–70.

Berggren, J. (2019). Writing, reviewing, and revising: Peer feedback in lower secondary EFL classrooms [Doctoral dissertation, Department of English, Stockholm University].

Bhowmik, S. K., Hilman, B., & Roy, S. (2019). Peer collaborative writing in the EAP classroom: Insights from a Canadian postsecondary context. *TESOL Journal, 10*(2), e00393. https://doi.org/10.1002/tesj.393.

Birjandi, P., & Hadidi Tamjid, N. (2012). The role of self-, peer and teacher assessment in promoting Iranian EFL learners' writing performance. *Assessment & Evaluation in Higher Education, 37*, 513–533. https://doi.org/10.1080/02602938.2010.549204.

Black, P., & Wiliam, D. (1998). Assessment and classroom learning. *Assessment in Education: Principles, Policy & Practice, 5*(1), 7–74. https://doi.org/10.1080/0969595980050102.

Black, P., & William, D. (2009). Developing the theory of formative assessment. *Educational Assessment, Evaluation and Accountability, 21*(1), 5–31. https://doi.org/10.1007/s11092-008-9068-5.

Blain, S. (2001). Study of verbal peer feedback on the improvement of the quality of writing and the transfer of knowledge in francophone students in grade 4 living in a minority situation in Canada. *Language Culture and Curriculum, 14*(2), 156–170. https://doi.org/10.1080/07908310108666619.

Boon, S. I. (2016). Increasing the uptake of peer feedback in primary school writing: Findings from an action research enquiry. *Education 3-13, 44*(2), 212–225.

Bouziane, A., & Zyad, H. (2018). The impact of self and peer assessment on L2 writing: The case of Moodle workshops. In A. Ahmed & H. Abouabdelkader (Eds.), *Assessing EFL writing in the 21st century Arab world* (pp. 111–135). Palgrave Macmillan. https://doi.org/10.1007/978-3-319-64104-1_5.

Jager, S., Bradley, Meima, E. J., & Thouësny, S. (Eds.) (2014). CALL design: Principles and practice. In *Proceedings of the 2014 EUROCALL Conference* (pp. 368–373), Groningen, The Netherlands. Research-publishing.net.

Bueno-Alastuey, M. C., Vasseur, R., & Elola, I. (2022). Effects of collaborative writing and peer feedback on Spanish as a foreign language writing performance. *Foreign Language Annals, 55*, 517–539. https://doi.org/10.1111/flan.12611.

Bui, G., & Kong, A. (2019). Metacognitive instruction for peer review inter-action in L2 writing. *Journal of Writing Research, 11*(2), 357–392. https://doi.org/10.17239/jowr-2019.11.02.05.

Caffarella, R. S., & Barnett, B. G. (2000). Teaching doctoral students to become scholarly writers: The importance of giving and receiving critiques. *Studies in Higher Education, 25*(1), 39–52. https://doi.org/10.1080/030750700116000.

Cao, S. Y., Zhou, S. R., Luo, Y., et al. (2022). A review of the ESL/EFL learners' gains from online peer feedback on English writing. *Frontiers in Psychology*, *13*. https://doi.org/10.3389/fpsyg.2022.1035803.

Cao, Z. H., Yu, S. L., & Huang, J. (2019). A qualitative inquiry into undergraduates' learning from giving and receiving peer feedback in L2 writing: Insights from a case study. *Studies in Educational Evaluation*, *63*, 102–112. https://doi.org/10.1016/j.stueduc.2019.08.001.

Carless, D. (2007). Conceptualizing pre-emptive formative assessment. *Assessment in Education: Principles, Policy & Practice*, *14*(2), 171–184. https://doi.org/10.1080/09695940701478412.

Carson, J. G., & Nelson, G. L. (1994). Writing groups: Cross-cultural issues. *Journal of Second Language Writing*, *3*(1), 17–30. https://doi.org/10.1016/1060-3743(94)90003-5.

Chang, C. Y. H. (2016). Two decades of research in L2 peer review. *Journal of Writing Research*, *8*(1), 81–117. https://doi.org/10.17239/jowr-2016.08.01.03.

Chen, C. H. (2010). The implementation and evaluation of a mobile self-and peer-assessment system. *Computers & Education*, *55*(1), 229–236. https://doi.org/10.1016/j.compedu.2010.01.008.

Chen, M., & Cui, Y. Q. (2022). The effects of AWE and peer feedback on cohesion and coherence in continuation writing. *Journal of Second Language Writing*, *57*. https://doi.org/10.1016/j.jslw.2022.100915.

Chen, T. (2016). Technology-supported peer feedback in ESL/EFL writing classes: A research synthesis. *Computer Assisted Language Learning*, *29*(2), 365–397. https://doi.org/10.1080/09588221.2014.960942.

Cheng, K. H., Liang, J. C., & Tsai, C. C. (2015). Examining the role of feedback messages in undergraduate students' writing performance during an online peer assessment activity. *The Internet and Higher Education*, *25*, 78–84. https://doi.org/10.1016/j.iheduc.2015.02.001.

Chin, C. K., Gong, C., & Tay, B. P. (2015). The effects of wiki-based recursive process writing on Chinese narrative essays for Chinese as a Second Language (CSL) students in Singapore. *IAFOR Journal of Education*, *3*(1), 45–59.

Cho, K., & MacArthur, C. (2010). Student revision with peer and expert reviewing. *Learning and Instruction*, *20*(4), 328–338. https://doi.org/10.1016/j.learninstruc.2009.08.006.

Cho, K., Schunn, C. D., & Charney, D. (2006). Commenting on writing: Typology and perceived helpfulness of comments from novice peer reviewers and subject matter experts. *Written Communication*, *23*(3), 260–294. https://doi.org/10.1177/0741088306289261.

Cho, K., Schunn, C. D., & Wilson, R. W. (2006). Validity and reliability of scaffolded peer assessment of writing from instructor and student perspectives. *Journal of Educational Psychology, 98*(4), 891–901. https://doi.org/10.1037/0022-0663.98.4.891.

Cho, Y. H., & Cho, K. (2011). Peer reviewers learn from giving comments. *Instructional Science, 39*(5), 629–643. https://doi.org/10.1007/s11251-010-9146-1.

Chong, S. W. (2018). Three paradigms of classroom assessment: Implications for written feedback research. *Language Assessment Quarterly,* 15(4), 330–347. https://doi.org/10.1080/15434303.2017.1405423.

Ciampa, K., & Wolfe, Z. M. (2023). From isolation to collaboration: Creating an intentional community of practice within the doctoral dissertation proposal writing process. *Teaching in Higher Education, 28*(3), 487–503. https://doi.org/10.1080/13562517.2020.1822313

Covill, A. E. (2010). Comparing peer review and self-review as ways to improve college students' writing. *Journal of Literacy Research, 42*(2), 199–226. https://doi.org/10.1080/10862961003796207.

Crinon, J. (2012). The dynamics of writing and peer review at primary school. *Journal of Writing Research, 4*(2), 121–154.

Cui, Y., Schunn, C. D., Gai, X. S., Jiang, Y., & Wang, Z. (2022). Effects of trained peer vs. teacher feedback on EFL students' writing performance, self-efficacy, and internalization of motivation. *Frontiers in Psychology, 13*, 788474. https://doi.org/10.3389/fpsyg.2022.878147.

Dann, R. (2014). Assessment *as* learning: Blurring the boundaries of assessment and learning for theory, policy and Practice. *Assessment in Education: Principles, Policy & Practice, 21*(2), 149–166. https://doi.org/10.1080/0969594x.2014.898128.

Double, K. S., McGrane, J. A., & Hopfenbeck, T. N. (2020). The impact of peer assessment on academic performance: A meta-analysis of control group studies. *Educational Psychology Review, 32*, 481–509.

Earl, L. M. (2013). *Assessment as learning: Using classroom assessment to maximize student learning.* Corwin Press.

Egan, A., & Costello, L. (2016). Peer assessment of, for and as learning: A core component of an accredited professional development course for Higher Education teachers. *All Ireland Journal of Higher Education, 8*(3), 2931–29313. http://ojs.aishe.org/index.php/aishe-j/article/view/293.

Esfandiari, R., & Myford, C. M. (2013). Severity differences among self-assessors, peer-assessors, and teacher assessors rating EFL essays. *Assessing Writing, 18*(2), 111–131. https://doi.org/10.1016/j.asw.2012.12.002.

Fan, Y., & Xu, J. (2020). Exploring student engagement with peer feedback on L2 writing. *Journal of Second Language Writing, 50*, 100775.

Ferguson, T. (2009). The "write" skills and more: A thesis writing group for doctoral students. *Journal of Geography in Higher Education, 33*(2), 285–297. https://doi.org/10.1080/03098260902734968.

Franco Ponce, R. M., Córdova Reyes, W. M., & Maloney, D. (2021). *Effectiveness of integrating ICTs in trained peer-review techniques: Improvement in ecuadorian secondary efl learners' quality of writing* [Doctoral dissertation, ESPOL. FCNM].

Gao, X., Asmawi, A., & Samuel, M. (2017). Critical peer feedback for business English writing through Qzone blogs: A mechanism among Chinese undergraduates. *GEMA Online Journal of Language Studies, 17*(1), 39–54. http://doi.org/10.17576/gema-2017-1701-03.

Geithner, C. A., & Pollastro, A. N. (2016). Doing peer review and receiving feedback: Impact on scientific literacy and writing skills. *Advances in Physiology Education, 40*(1), 38–46. https://doi.org/10.1152/advan.00071.2015.

Han, Y., & Hyland, F. (2015). Exploring learner engagement with written corrective feedback in a Chinese tertiary EFL classroom. *Journal of Second Language Writing, 30*, 31–44.

Harris, L. R., Brown, G. T., & Harnett, J. A. (2015). Analysis of New Zealand primary and secondary student peer-and self-assessment comments: Applying Hattie and Timperley's feedback model. *Assessment in Education: Principles, Policy & Practice, 22*(2), 265–281.

Heift, T., & Caws, C. (2000). Peer feedback in synchronous writing environments: A case study in French. *Educational Technology & Society, 3*(3), 208–214. www.jstor.org/stable/10.2307/jeductechsoci.3.3.208.

Hu, G. (2005). Using peer review with Chinese ESL student writers. *Language Teaching Research, 9*(3), 321–342. https://doi.org/10.1191/1362168805 lr169oa.

Huang, S. C. (2015). Setting writing revision goals after assessment for learning. *Language Assessment Quarterly, 12*(4), 363–385.

Huisman, B., Saab, N., van Driel, J., & van den Broek, P. (2017). Peer feedback on college students' writing: Exploring the relation between students' ability match, feedback quality and essay performance. *Higher Education Research & Development, 36*(7), 1433–1447. https://doi.org/10.1080/07294360.2017 .1325854.

Huisman, B., Saab, N., van Driel, J., & Van Den Broek, P. (2018). Peer feedback on academic writing: Undergraduate students' peer feedback role, peer feedback perceptions and essay performance. *Assessment & Evaluation in Higher Education, 43*(6), 955–968. https://doi.org/10.1080/02602938.2018.1424318.

Hyland, F. (2000). ESL writers and feedback: Giving more autonomy to students. *Language Teaching Research, 4*(1), 33–54.

Hyland, K., & Hyland, F. (2006). Feedback on second language students' writing. *Language Teaching*, *39*(2), 83–101. https://doi.org/10.1017/S0261444806003399.

Illana-Mahiques, E. (2021). Re-thinking peer reviewing in the virtual context: The roles of giving and receiving online feedback in L2 Spanish classrooms. *Languages*, *6*(3), 151. https://doi.org/10.3390/languages6030151.

Jogan, M. K., Ana, H. H., & Gladys, A. M. (2001). Cross-cultural e-mail: Providing cultural input for the advanced foreign language student. *Foreign Language Annals*, *34*(4), 341–346. https://doi.org/10.1111/j.1944-9720.2001.tb02066.x.

Kim, H. (2012). *Writing, peer feedback, and revision : A comparison of L1 and L2 college freshmen with longitudinal analyses* [Doctoral dissertation, The University of Texas at Austin]. http://hdl.handle.net/2152/28468.

Kinginger, C., & Belz, J. (2005). Socio-cultural perspectives on pragmatic development in foreign language learning: Microgenetic case studies from telecollaboration and residence abroad. *Intercultural Pragmatics*, *2*(4), 369–421. https://doi.org/10.1515/iprg.2005.2.4.369.

Kumar, V., & Stracke, E. (2011). Examiners' reports on theses: Feedback or assessment?. *Journal of English for Academic Purposes*, *10*(4), 211–222. https://doi.org/10.1016/j.jeap.2011.06.001.

Lam, R. (2013). The relationship between assessment types and text revision. *ELT Journal*, *67*(4), 446–458. https://doi.org/10.1093/elt/cct034.

Lam, R. (2016). Assessment as learning: Examining a cycle of teaching, learning, and assessment of writing in the portfolio-based classroom. *Studies in Higher Education*, *41*(11), 1900–1917. https://doi.org/10.1080/03075079.2014.999317.

Latifi, S., Noroozi, O., Hatami, J., & Biemans, H. J. (2021). How does online peer feedback improve argumentative essay writing and learning? *Innovations in Education and Teaching International*, *58*(2), 195–206.

Lee, I. (2007). Feedback in Hong Kong secondary writing classrooms: Assessment for learning or assessment of learning?. *Assessing Writing*, *12*(3), 180–198. https://doi.org/10.1016/j.asw.2008.02.003.

Lee, I. (2011). Formative assessment in EFL writing: An exploratory case study. *Changing English*, *18*(1), 99–111. https://doi.org/10.1080/1358684X.2011.543516.

Lee, I. (2017). *Classroom assessment and feedback in L2 school contexts*. Singapore: Springer.

Lee, I., & Coniam, D. (2013). Introducing assessment for learning for EFL writing in an assessment of learning examination-driven system in Hong

Kong. *Journal of Second Language Writing, 22*(1), 34–50. https://doi.org/10.1016/j.jslw.2012.11.003.

Lee, I., Mak, P., & Yuan, R. (2019). Assessment as learning in primary writing classrooms: An exploratory study. *Studies in Educational Evaluation, 62*, 72–81.

Lee, M. K. (2015). Peer feedback in second language writing: Investigating junior secondary students' perspectives on inter-feedback and intra-feedback. *System*, 55, 1–10. https://doi.org/10.1016/j.system.2015.08.003.

Lee, M., & Evans, M. (2019). Investigating the operating mechanisms of the sources of L2 writing self-efficacy at the stages of giving and receiving peer feedback. *Modern Language Journal, 103*(4), 831–847. https://doi.org/10.1111/modl.12598.

Leung, K., Chan, M., Maxwell, G., & Poon, T. (2010). A qualitative analysis of sub-degree students commentary styles and patterns in the context of gender and peer e-feedback. In *Hybrid Learning: Third International Conference, ICHL 2010, Beijing, China, August 16–18, 2010. Proceedings 3* (pp. 149–159). Springer Berlin Heidelberg.

Li, L., Liu, X., & Steckelberg, A. L. (2010). Assessor or assessee: How student learning improves by giving and receiving peer feedback. *British Journal of Educational Technology, 41*(3), 525–536. https://doi.org/10.1111/j.1467-8535.2009.00968.x.

Li, X., Xia, Q., Chu, S. K. W., & Yang, Y. (2022). Using gamification to facilitate students' self-regulation in e-learning: A case study on students' L2 English learning. *Sustainability, 14*(12), 7008.

Lin, C.-J. (2019). An online peer assessment approach to supporting mind-mapping flipped learning activities for college English writing courses. *Journal of Computers in Education, 6*, 385–415. https://doi.org/10.1007/s40692-019-00144-6.

Lin, S. S., Liu, E. Z. F., & Yuan, S. M. (2001). Web-based peer assessment: feedback for students with various thinking-styles. *Journal of Computer assisted Learning, 17*(4), 420–432. https://doi.org/10.1046/j.0266-4909.2001.00198.

Lindgren, R. (2018). "The main thing with peer review, if we help each other out, that is a quicker way to get a better result": Teachers' experience of using peer review in the English classroom. Malmö University.

Liu, J., & Hansen Edwards, J. (2002). *Peer response in second language writing classrooms*. University of Michigan Press.

Liu, X., Li, L., & Zhang, Z. (2018). Small group discussion as a key component in online assessment training for enhanced student learning in web-based peer assessment. *Assessment and Evaluation in Higher Education*, *43*(2), 207–222. https://doi.org/10.1080/02602938.2017.1324018.

López-Pellisa, T., Rotger, N., & Rodríguez-Gallego, F. (2020). Collaborative writing at work: Peer feedback in a blended learning environment. *Education and Information Technologies*, *26*(1), 1293–1310. https://doi.org/10.1007/s10639-020-10312-2.

Lu, Q., Zhu, X. H., & Cheong, C. M. (2021). Understanding the difference between self-feedback and peer feedback: A comparative study of their effects on undergraduate students' writing improvement. *Frontiers in Psychology*, *12*. https://doi.org/10.3389/fpsyg.2021.739962.

Ludemann, P. M., & McMakin, D. (2014). Perceived helpfulness of peer editing activities: First-year students' views and writing performance outcomes. *Psychology Learning & Teaching*, *13*(2), 129–136. https://doi.org/10.2304/plat.2014.13.2.129.

Ma, Q. (2020). Examining the role of inter-group peer online feedback on wiki writing in an EAP context. *Computer Assisted Language Learning*, *33*(3), 197-216. https://doi.org/10.1080/09588221.2018.1556703.

Mao, Z., & Lee, I. (2022). Researching L2 student engagement with written feedback: Insights from sociocultural theory. *TESOL Quarterly*, *56*(2), 788–798.

Mao, Z., & Lee, I. (2023). Student engagement with written feedback: Critical issues and way forward. *RELC Journal*, 00336882221150811.

Man, D., Xu, Y., & O'Toole, J. M. (2018). Understanding autonomous peer feedback practices among postgraduate students: A case study in a Chinese university. *Assessment & Evaluation in Higher Education*, *43*(4), 527–536. https://doi.org/10.1080/02602938.2017.1376310.

McConlogue, T. (2015). Making judgements: Investigating the process of composing and receiving peer feedback. *Studies in Higher Education*, *40*, 1495–1506.

McDonough, K., Ammar, A., & Michaud, G. (2022). L2 peer interaction before and after writing: How does each one promote writing development? *The Canadian Modern Language Review*, *78*(1), 1-16. https://doi.org/10.3138/cmlr-2020-0073.

McDonough, K., Ammar, A., & Sellami, A. (2021). L2 French students' conversations during interactive writing tasks and their interaction mindset. *Foreign Language Annuals*, *55*(1), 222–236. https://doi.org/10.1111/flan.12594.

McIsaac, C. M., & Sepe, J. F. (1996). Improving the writing of accounting students: A cooperative venture. *Journal of Accounting Education*, *14*(4), 515–533. https://doi.org/10.1016/S0748-5751(96)00027-9.

Meek, S. E., Blakemore, L., & Marks, L. (2017). Is peer review an appropriate form of assessment in a MOOC? Student participation and performance in formative peer review. *Assessment & Evaluation in Higher Education*, *42*(6), 1000–1013. https://doi.org/10.1080/02602938.2016.1221052.

Meletiadou, E. (2021a). Exploring the impact of peer assessment on EFL students' writing performance. *IAFOR Journal of Education: Language Learning in Education*, *9*(3), 78–95. https://doi.org/10.22492/ije.9.3.05.

Meletiadou, E. (2021b). Opening Pandora's box: How does peer assessment affect EFL students' writing quality? *Languages*, *6*(115), 1–17. https://doi.org/10.3390/languages6030115.

Miao, Y., Badger, R., & Zhen, Y. (2006). A comparative study of peer and teacher feedback in a Chinese EFL writing class. *Journal of Second Language Writing*, *15*(3), 179–200. https://doi.org/10.1016/j.jslw.2006.09.004.

Min, H. T. (2006). The effects of trained peer review on EFL students' revision types and writing quality. *Journal of Second Language Writing*, *15*(2), 118–141. https://doi.org/10.1016/j.jslw.2006.01.003.

Min, H. T. (2018). Trained peer written feedback and teacher written feedback: Similar or different? *English Teaching & Learning*, *42*(2), 131–153. https://doi.org/10.1007/s42321-018-0009-1.

Nelson, G. L., & Carson, J. G. (1998). ESL students' perceptions of effectiveness in peer response groups. *Journal of Second Language Writing*, *7*, 113–131.

Nelson, M. M., & Schunn, C. D. (2009). The nature of feedback: How different types of peer feedback affect writing performance. *Instructional Science*, *37*(4), 375–401. https://doi.org/10.1007/s11251-008-9053-x.

Nguyen, T. T. M. (2008). Modifying L2 criticisms: How learners do it?. *Journal of Pragmatics*, *40*(4), 768–791.

Nguyen, T. T. L. (2018). The effect of combined peer-teacher feedback on Thai students' writing accuracy. *Iranian Journal of Language Teaching Research*, *6*(2), 117–132.

Nicolaidou. (2013). E-portfolios supporting primary students' writing performance and peer feedback. *Computers and Education*, *68*, 404–415. https://doi.org/10.1016/j.compedu.2013.06.004

O'Donnell, M. E. (2014). Peer response with process-oriented, standards-based writing for beginning-level, second language learners of Spanish. *Hispania*, *97*(3), 413–429. www.jstor.org/stable/24368817.

Ozkul, A. (2017). *Peer response in L1 writing: Impact on revisons and student perceptions*. [Master's thesis, Iowa State University]. https://lib.dr.iastate.edu/etd/15394.

Pajares, F. (2003). Self-efficacy beliefs, motivation, and achievement in writing: A review of the literature. *Reading & Writing Quarterly, 19*(2), 139–158. https://doi.org/10.1080/10573560308222.

Panadero, E., & Alqassab, M. (2019). An empirical review of anonymity effects in peer assessment, peer feedback, peer review, peer evaluation and peer grading. *Assessment and Evaluation in Higher Education, 44*(8), 1253–1278. https://doi.org/10.1080/02602938.2019.1600186.

Patchan, M. M., Charney, D., & Schunn, C. D. (2009). A validation study of students' end comments: Comparing comments by students, a writing instructor, and a content instructor. *Journal of Writing Research, 1*(2), 124–152. www.jowr.org/pkp/ojs/index.php/jowr/article/view/753.

Patchan, M. M., Schunn, C. D., & Clark, R. J. (2011). Writing in the natural sciences: Understanding the effects of different types of reviewers on the writing process. *Journal of Writing Research, 2*(3), 365–393.

Peterson, S. S., & McClay, J. (2010). Assessing and providing feedback for student writing in Canadian classrooms. *Assessing Writing, 15*(2), 86–99. https://doi.org/10.1016/j.asw.2010.05.003.

Peterson, S. S., & Portier, C. (2014). Grade one peer and teacher feedback on student writing. *Education 3–13, 42*(3), 237–257. https://doi.org/10.1080/03004279.2012.670256.

Pham, H. T. P. (2022). Computer-mediated and face-to-face peer feedback: Student feedback and revision in EFL writing. *Computer Assisted Language Learning, 35*(9), 2112–2147. https://doi.org/10.1080/09588221.2020.1868530.

Pham, T. N., Lin, M., Trinh, V. Q., & Bui, L. T. P. (2020). Electronic peer feedback, EFL academic writing and reflective thinking: Evidence from a Confucian context. *Sage Open, 10*(1). https://doi.org/10.1177/2158244020914554.

Pope, N. (2001). An examination of the use of peer rating for formative assessment in the context of the theory of consumption values. *Assessment & Evaluation in Higher Education, 26*, 235–246. https://doi.org/10.1080/02602930120052396.

Ramon-Casas, M., Nuño, N., Pons, F., & Cunillera, T. (2019). The different impact of a structured peer-assessment task in relation to university undergraduates' initial writing skills. *Assessment & Evaluation in Higher Education, 44*(5), 653–663. https://doi.org/10.1080/02602938.2018.1525337.

Rezai, A., Rahul, D. R., Asif, M., Omar, A., & Reshad Jamalyar, A. (2022). Contributions of E-portfolios assessment to developing EFL learners' vocabulary, motivation, and attitudes. *Education Research International, 2022*, 1–11. https://doi.org/10.1155/2022/5713278.

Roux-Rodriguez, R. (2003). *Computer-mediated peer response and its impact on revision in the college Spanish classroom: A case study.* University of South Florida.

Ruecker, T. (2010). The potential of dual-language cross-cultural peer review. *ELT Journal, 65*(4), 398-407. https://doi.org/10.1093/elt/ccq067.

Ruegg, R. (2015). The relative effects of peer and teacher feedback on improvement in EFL students' writing ability. *Linguistics and Education, 29*, 73–82. https://doi.org/10.1016/j.linged.2014.12.001.

Ruegg, R. (2010). Aspects affecting confidence in writing. *Studies in Linguistics and Language Teaching, 21*, 123–135.

Ruegg, R. (2018). The effect of peer and teacher feedback on changes in EFL students' writing self-efficacy. *Language Learning Journal, 46*(2), 87–102. https://doi.org/10.1080/09571736.2014.958190.

Sadeghi, K., & Rahmati, T. (2017). Integrating assessment as, for, and of learning in a large-scale exam preparation course. *Assessing Writing, 34*, 50–61. https://doi.org/10.1016/j.asw.2017.09.003.

Sadler, P. M., & Good, E. (2006). The impact of self- and peer-grading on student learning. *Educational Assessment, 11*(1), 1–31.

Saeed, M. A., Ghazali, K., & Aljaberi, M. A. (2018). A review of previous studies on ESL/EFL learners' interactional feedback exchanges in face-to-face and computer-assisted peer review of writing. *International Journal of Educational Technology in Higher Education, 15*. https://doi.org/10.1186/s41239-017-0084-8.

Saeed, M. A., Ghazali, K., Sahuri, S. S., & Abdulrab, M. (2018). Engaging EFL learners in online peer feedback on writing: What does it tell us? *Journal of Information Technology Education-Research, 17*, 39–61. https://doi.org/10.28945/3980.

Saito, H., & Fujita, T. (2004). Characteristics and user acceptance of peer rating in EFL writing classrooms. *Language Teaching Research, 8*(1), 31–54. https://doi.org/10.1191/1362168804lr133o.

Sánchez-Naranjo, J. (2019). Peer review and training: Pathways to quality and value in second language writing. *Foreign Language Annals, 52*(3), 612–643. https://doi.org/10.1111/flan.12414.

Schellekens, L. H., Bok, H. G. J., de Jong, L. H., et al. (2021). A scoping review on the notions of assessment as learning (AAL), assessment for learning (AFL), and assessment of learning (AOL). *Studies in Educational Evaluation, 71*, 101094. https://doi.org/10.1016/j.stueduc.2021.101094.

Schunk, D. H., & Swartz, C. W. (1993). Writing strategy instruction with gifted students: Effects of goals and feedback on self-efficacy and skills. *Roeper Review, 15*(4), 225–230. https://doi.org/10.1080/02783199309553512.

Schunn, C., Godley, A., & DeMartino, S. (2016). The reliability and validity of peer review of writing in high school AP English classes. *Journal of Adolescent & Adult Literacy, 60*(1), 13–23. https://doi.org/10.1002/jaal.525.

Serafini, F. (2001). Three paradigms of assessment: Measurement, procedure, and inquiry. *The Reading Teacher, 54*(4), 384–393.

Shang, H. F. (2022). Exploring online peer feedback and automated corrective feedback on EFL writing performance. *Interactive Learning Environments, 30*(1), 4–16. https://doi.org/10.1080/10494820.2019.1629601.

Shen, B., Bai, B., & Xue, W. (2020). The effects of peer assessment on learner autonomy: An empirical study in a Chinese college English writing class. *Studies in Educational Evaluation, 64*, 1–10.

Snyder, D. W., Nielson, R. P., & Kurzer, K. (2016). Foreign language writing fellows programs: A model for improving advanced writing skills. *Foreign Language Annals, 49*(4), 750–771. https://doi.org/10.1111/flan.12231.

Strijbos, J. W., Narciss, S., & Dünnebier, K. (2010). Peer feedback content and sender's competence level in academic writing revision tasks: Are they critical for feedback perceptions and efficiency?. *Learning and Instruction, 20*(4), 291–303. https://doi.org/10.1016/j.learninstruc.2009.08.008.

Strobl, C. (2014). Affordances of Web 2.0 technologies for collaborative advanced writing in a foreign language. *Calico Journal, 31*(1), 1–18.

Sun, H. Y., & Wang, M. C. (2022). Effects of teacher intervention and type of peer feedback on student writing revision. *Language Teaching Research.* https://doi.org/10.1177/13621688221080507.

Sun, P. P., & Jun Zhang, L. (2022). Effects of translanguaging in online peer feedback on Chinese University English-as-a-foreign-language students' writing performance. *RELC Journal, 53*(2), 325–341. https://doi.org/10.1177/00336882221089051.

Sutton, P. (2012). Conceptualizing feedback literacy: Knowing, being, and acting. *Innovations in Education and Teaching International, 49*(1), 31–40.

Tai, H. C., Lin, W. C., & Yang, S. C. (2015). Exploring the effects of peer review and teachers' corrective feedback on EFL students' online writing performance. *Journal of Educational Computing Research, 53*(2), 284–309. https://doi.org/10.1177/0735633115597490.

Tan, S. X., Cho, Y. W., & Xu, W. S. (2022). Exploring the effects of automated written corrective feedback, computer-mediated peer feedback and their combination mode on EFL learner's writing performance. *Interactive Learning Environments.* https://doi.org/10.1080/10494820.2022.2066137.

Tharp, R. G., & Gallimore, R. (1988). *Rousing minds to life: Teaching, learning, and schooling in social context.* Cambridge University Press.

Tian, J. (2011). The effects of peer editing versus co-writing on writing in Chinese-as-a-foreign language [Doctoral dissertation, University of Victoria].

Tian, L. L., Liu, Q. S., & Zhang, X. X. (2022). Self-regulated writing strategy use when revising upon automated, peer, and teacher feedback in an online English as a foreign language writing course. *Frontiers in Psychology, 13.* https://doi.org/10.3389/fpsyg.2022.873170.

Topping, K. (1998). Peer assessment between students in colleges and universities. *Review of Educational Research, 68*(3), 249–276. https://doi.org/10.3102/00346543068003249.

Topping, K. J. (2009). Peer assessment. *Theory into Practice, 48*(1), 20–27.

Topping, K. J. (2017). Peer assessment: Learning by judging and discussing the work of other learners. *Interdisciplinary Education and Psychology, 1*(1), 7. https://doi.org/10.31532/interdiscipeducpsychol.1.1.007.

Topping, K. J., Smith, E. F., Swanson, I., & Elliot, A. (2000). Formative peer assessment of academic writing between postgraduate students. *Assessment & Evaluation in Higher Education, 25*(2), 149–169. https://doi.org/10.1080/713611428.

Tran, O. T. T., & Pham, V. P. H. (2023). The effects of online peer feedback on students' writing skills during corona virus pandemic. *International Journal of Instruction, 16*(1), 881–896. https://doi.org/10.29333/iji.2023.16149a.

Tsagari, D., & Meletiadou, E. (2015). Peer assessment of adolescent learners' writing performance. *Writing & Pedagogy, 7.* https://doi.org/10.1558/wap.v7i2-3.26457.

Tsui, A. B., & Ng, M. (2000). Do secondary L2 writers benefit from peer comments?. *Journal of Second Language Writing, 9*(2), 147–170. https://doi.org/10.1016/S1060-3743(00)00022-9.

Tunagür, M. (2021). The effect of peer assessment application on writing anxiety and writing motivation of 6th grade students. *Shanlax International Journal of Education, 10*(1), 96–105. https://doi.org/10.34293/education.v10i1.4352.

Venables, A., & Summit, R. (2003). Enhancing scientific essay writing using peer assessment. *Innovations in Education and Teaching International, 40*(3), 281–290. https://doi.org/10.1080/1470329032000103816.

Vorobel, O. (2013). A case study of peer review practices of four adolescent English language learners in face-to-face and online contexts. [Doctoral dissertation, University of South Florida].

Vougan, A., & Li, S. (2023). Examining the effectiveness of peer feedback in second language writing: A meta-analysis. *TESOL Quarterly, 57*(4), 1115–1138.

Wanner, T., & Palmer, E. (2018). Formative self-and peer assessment for improved student learning: The crucial factors of design, teacher participation and feedback. *Assessment & Evaluation in Higher Education*, *43*(7), 1032–1047. https://doi.org/10.1080/02602938.2018.1427698.

Ware, P., & O'Dowd, R. (2008). Peer feedback on language form in telecollaboration. *Language Learning & Technology*, *12*(1), 43–63. http://llt.msu.edu/vol12num1/wareodowd/.

Warschauer, M., & Grimes, D. (2007). Audience, authorship, and artifact: The emergent semiotics of Web 2.0. *Annual Review of Applied Linguistics*, *27*, 1–23. https://doi.org/10.1017/S0267190508070013.

Wei, W., Cheong, C. M., Zhu, X. H., & Lu, Q. (2022). Comparing self-reflection and peer feedback practices in an academic writing task: A student self-efficacy perspective. *Teaching in Higher Education*. https://doi.org/10.1080/13562517.2022.2042242.

Wichmann, A., Funk, A., & Rummel, N. (2018). Leveraging the potential of peer feedback in an academic writing activity through sense-making support. *European Journal of Psychology of Education*, *33*, 165–184. https://doi.org/10.1007/s10212-017-0348-7.

Wiliam, D. (2006). Formative assessment: Getting the focus right. *Educational Assessment*, *11*(3–4), 283–289.

Woo, M. M., Chu, S. K. W., & Li, X. (2013). Peer-feedback and revision process in a wiki mediated collaborative writing. *Educational Technology Research and Development*, *61*, 279–309. https://doi.org/10.1007/s11423-012-9285-y.

Woodhouse, J., & Wood, P. (2022). Creating dialogic spaces: Developing doctoral students' critical writing skills through peer assessment and review *Studies in Higher Education*, *47*(3), 643–655. https://doi.org/10.1080/03075079.2020.1779686.

Wooley, R. S. (2007). *The effects of web-based peer review on student writing* [Doctoral dissertation, Kent State University].

Wu, L. (2009). Understanding SLA through peer interactions in a Chinese classroom: A sociocultural perspective [Doctoral dissertation, University of New Hampshire].

Wu, W. Y., Huang, J. Y., Han, C. W., & Zhang, J. (2022). Evaluating peer feedback as a reliable and valid complementary aid to teacher feedback in EFL writing classrooms: A feedback giver perspective. *Studies in Educational Evaluation*, *73*. https://doi.org/10.1016/j.stueduc.2022.101140.

Wu, Y., & Schunn, C. D. (2023). Passive, active, and constructive engagement with peer feedback: A revised model of learning from peer feedback. *Contemporary Educational Psychology*, 102160. https://doi.org/10.1016/j.cedpsych.2023.102160.

Xiao, Y., & Lucking, R. (2008). The impact of two types of peer assessment on students' performance and satisfaction within a Wiki environment. *The Internet and Higher Education, 11*(3–4), 186–193. https://doi.org/10.1016/j.iheduc.2008.06.005.

Yang, Y. F. (2016). Transforming and constructing academic knowledge through online peer feedback in summary writing. *Computer Assisted Language Learning, 29*(4), 683–702. https://doi.org/10.1080/09588221.2015.1016440.

Yu, S. (2019). Learning from giving peer feedback on postgraduate theses: Voices from Master's students in the Macau EFL context. *Assessing Writing, 40*, 42–52. https://doi.org/10.1016/j.asw.2019.03.004.

Yu, S., & Hu, G. (2017). Can higher-proficiency L2 learners benefit from working with lower-proficiency partners in peer feedback?. *Teaching in Higher Education, 22*(2), 178–192.

Yu, S., & Lee, I. (2014). An analysis of Chinese EFL students' use of first and second language in peer feedback of L2 writing. *System, 47*, 28–38. https://doi.org/10.1016/j.system.2014.08.007.

Yu, S., & Lee, I. (2016a). Peer feedback in second language writing (2005–2014). *Language Teaching, 49*(4), 461–493. https://doi.org/10.1017/S0261444816000161.

Yu, S., & Lee, I. (2016b). Understanding the role of learners with low English language proficiency in peer feedback of second language writing. *TESOL Quarterly, 50*(2), 483–494. www.jstor.org/stable/43893831.

Yu, S., & Liu, C. (2021). Improving student feedback literacy in academic writing: An evidence-based framework. *Assessing Writing, 48*, 100525.

Yu, S., Zhang, Y., Zheng, Y., Yuan, K., & Zhang, L. (2019). Understanding student engagement with peer feedback on master's theses: A Macau study. *Assessment & Evaluation in Higher Education, 44*(1), 50–65. https://doi.org/10.1080/02602938.2018.1467879.

Zaccaron, R., & Xhafaj, D. C. (2020). Knowing me, knowing you: A comparative study on the effects of anonymous and conference peer feedback on the writing of learners of English as an additional language. *System, 95*(4), 102367. https://doi.org/10.1016/j.system.2020.102367.

Zhang, M., He, Q., Du, J., Liu, F., & Huang, B. (2022). Learners' perceived advantages and social-affective dispositions toward online peer feedback in academic writing. *Frontiers in Psychology, 13*, 973478. https://doi.org/10.3389/fpsyg.2022.973478.

Zhang, R. F., & Zou, D. (2022). A review of research on technology-enhanced peer feedback for second language writing based on the activity theory framework. *Education and Information Technologies*. https://doi.org/10.1007/s10639-022-11469-8.

Zhang, S. (1995). Reexamining the affective advantage of peer feedback in the ESL writing class. *Journal of Second Language Writing, 4*, 209–222.

Zhang, X., & McEneaney, J. E. (2020). What is the influence of peer feedback and author response on Chinese university students' English writing performance? *Reading Research Quarterly, 55*(1), 123–146. https://doi.org/10.1002/rrq.259.

Zhang, X. D., & Yu, S. L. (2022). Training student writers in conducting peer feedback in L2 writing: A meaning-making perspective. *Applied Linguistics Review, 13*(4), 439–460. https://doi.org/10.1515/applirev-2019-0045.

Zhang, Z. (2017). Student engagement with computer-generated feedback: A case study. *ELT Journal, 71*(3), 317–328.

Zhang, Z. V., & Hyland, K. (2018). Student engagement with teacher and automated feedback on L2 writing. *Assessing Writing, 36*, 90–102.

Zheng, Y., & Yu, S. (2018). Student engagement with teacher written corrective feedback in EFL writing: A case study of Chinese lower-proficiency students. *Assessing Writing, 37*, 13–24.

Zhao, H. (2018). Exploring tertiary English as a Foreign Language writing tutors' perceptions of the appropriateness of peer assessment for writing. *Assessment & Evaluation in Higher Education, 43*(7), 1133–1145. https://doi.org/10.1080/02602938.2018.1434610.

Zheng, L. Q., Cui, P. P., Li, X., & Huang, R. H. (2018). Synchronous discussion between assessors and assessees in web-based peer assessment: Impact on writing performance, feedback quality, meta-cognitive awareness and self-efficacy. *Assessment & Evaluation in Higher Education, 43*(3), 500–514. https://doi.org/10.1080/02602938.2017.1370533.

Zhou, J., Zheng, Y., & Tai, J. H.-M. (2020). Grudges and gratitude: The social-affective impacts of peer assessment. *Assessment & Evaluation in Higher Education, 45*(3), 345–358. https://doi.org/10.1080/02602938.2019.1643449.

Zimmerman, B. J., & Schunk, D. H. (2008). Motivation: An essential dimension of self-regulated learning. In D. H. Schunk & B. J. Zimmerman (Eds.), *Motivation and self-regulated learning: Theory, research, and applications* (pp. 1–30). Lawrence Erlbaum Associates Publishers.

Zou, D., Xie, H. R., & Wang, F. L. (2022). Effects of technology enhanced peer, teacher and self-feedback on students' collaborative writing, critical thinking tendency and engagement in learning. *Journal of Computing in Higher Education*. https://doi.org/10.1007/s12528-022-09337.

Zou, Y., Schunn, C. D., Wang, Y., & Zhang, F. (2018). Student attitudes that predict participation in peer assessment. *Assessment & Evaluation in Higher Education, 43*(5), 800–811. https://doi.org/10.1080/02602938.2017.1409872.

Funding Statement

MYRG2022-00273-FED, University of Macau.

Cambridge Elements ⹅

Language Teaching

Heath Rose
University of Oxford

Heath Rose is Professor of Applied Linguistics at the University of Oxford.
At Oxford, he is the course director of the MSc in Applied Linguistics for Language Teaching.
Before moving into academia, Heath worked as a language teacher in Australia
and Japan in both school and university contexts. He is author of numerous books, such as
*Introducing Global Englishes, The Japanese Writing System, Data Collection Research
Methods in Applied Linguistics*, and *Global Englishes for Language Teaching*. Heath's research
interests are firmly situated within the field of second language teaching, and
includes work on Global Englishes, teaching English as an international language, and
English Medium Instruction.

Jim McKinley
University College London

Jim McKinley is Professor of Applied Linguistics and TESOL at UCL, Institute
of Education, where he serves as Academic Head of Learning and Teaching. His major
research areas are second language writing in global contexts, the internationalisation of
higher education, and the relationship between teaching and research. Jim has edited or
authored numerous books, including the *Routledge Handbook of Research
Methods in Applied Linguistics, Data Collection Research Methods in Applied Linguistics*, and
Doing Research in Applied Linguistics. He is also an editor of the journal, *System*. Before
moving into academia, Jim taught in a range of diverse contexts including the US,
Australia, Japan and Uganda.

Advisory Board
Brian Paltridge, *University of Sydney*
Gary Barkhuizen, *University of Auckland*
Marta Gonzalez-Lloret, *University of Hawaii*
Li Wei, *UCL Institute of Education*
Victoria Murphy, *University of Oxford*
Diane Pecorari, *University of Leeds*
Christa Van der *Walt, Stellenbosch University*
Yongyan Zheng, *Fudan University*

About the Series
This Elements series aims to close the gap between researchers and practitioners by allying
research with language teaching practices, in its exploration of research-informed
teaching, and teaching-informed research. The series builds upon a rich history
of pedagogical research in its exploration of new insights within the field
of language teaching.

Cambridge Elements ≡

Language Teaching

Printed in the United States
by Baker & Taylor Publisher Services